British Railways Picto

Crewe North

Alan Wilkinson

Ian Allan
PUBLISHING

CONTENTS

First published 2007

ISBN (10) 0 7110 3207 6
ISBN (13) 978 0 7110 3207 1

Published by Ian Allan Publishing

an imprint of Ian Allan Publishing Ltd, Hersham, Surrey KT12 4RG
Printed in England by Ian Allan Printing Ltd, Hersham, Surrey KT12 4RG

Code: 0710/B

Visit the Ian Allan Publishing website at www.ianallanpublishing.com

Acknowledgements

What a unique situation I find myself in. One where so many thanks are due and are duly acknowledged here. To all of you who have contributed to this book in whatever way: thank you. You were known to Alan and my sincere apologises for any omissions.
  The book is dedicated to all who love railways. Especial thanks are due to Clive Mojonnier – this book would not have happened without him – and to Alan himself for his inspiration and dedication to all things locomotive and steam-driven in particular.

Margaret Wilkinson
September 2007

Title page:
Hartford, milepost 170, *c*1947
This is what West Coast train viewing was all about! Stanier's 'Duchesses' were built to the limit of the loading gauge and exuded power and majesty unsurpassed (and unequalled!) by any other British locomotive. Just after the war No 6223 *Princess Alice* carries the last LMS lined-black passenger livery. Despite the 17-coach load and doubtful post-war conditions, she is clearly on top of the job as she pounds towards Hartford station with an up express. *G. W. Smith, Kidderminster Railway Museum 010431*

Left:
Acton Grange Junction, summer 1954
The setting sun highlights the majestic prospect of Crewe North 'Princess' No 46209 *Princess Beatrice* clearing the Ship Canal bridge and crossing the junction at the top of the 1 in 135 climb from Warrington with the 15-coach up 'Midday Scot' from Glasgow to Euston. *F. Wemyss-Smith, M. S. Welch collection*

INTRODUCTION

I was very lucky to grow up close to one of the country's oldest and most important trunk railways – the West Coast route to Scotland. From a very early age I was captivated by the enthralling sound of the overnight sleepers and merchandise freights echoing across the quiet Cheshire fields, and on Sunday afternoons in the mid-1950s I would willingly walk the 3 miles to Winsford station to see the up 'Royal Scot', invariably headed by a 'Duchess' Pacific – for me the very ultimate in British express power. My first school was just a field away from the line between Minshull Vernon and Winsford, and one morning I was found absent and quite oblivious to educational matters, standing on an appropriated dustbin enjoying the passing spectacle! Secondary school provided a clear view between Verdin Sidings and Winsford Junction, which in the era of change from steam to diesel, could be *very* distracting from lessons! And homeward-bound on a brilliant March afternoon in 1962 I saw *Princess Beatrice* for the last time, streaking through Winsford with the down 'Red Rose', just one of dozens of steam spectacles witnessed in the vicinity in those all too short years between 1958 and 1967.

A warm summer morning in 1958, lazing by the railway absorbing the aromas from the nearby farm and the distinctive smell of creosote from the wooden railway fences, communication troughs, sleepers, and the wonderful lines of telegraph poles that lined the railway in those days. '3F' 0-6-0 No 43464 is standing on the Down Slow with the 'Winsford Flyer' for Over & Wharton, followed by a 'Super D' 0-8-0 on a cattle special, then a 'Black Five' on a fitted freight and a Stanier 2-6-0 on a through freight, all waiting for a gap in the traffic to proceed to Winsford Junction. With the view of the main line now blocked, I pedal off along Clive Back Lane to a location just south of Winsford station, now rendered inaccessible by the latest 'penitentiary' fencing. A pulsatingly urgent staccato heralds the approach of an up express as No 46207 *Princess Arthur of Connaught* whistles imperiously for the station and storms by at 70mph with the 16-coach 'Merseyside Express' – similar spectacles being repeated throughout the day. This is some railway – passenger

trains to multifarious and scattered destinations, heavy merchandise freights galore, the occasional mineral or tank train, parcels and infrequent locals. Schoolboy knowledge of world geography, British colonies and Army regiments is constantly reinforced by the daily procession of named '5X' and '7P' 4-6-0s, trains at five-minute intervals and virtually all steam-powered. Wherever else would one wish to be in the school holidays?

Our presence at Winsford on the station bridge or on the supports of a large poster hoarding alongside the up platform was not always appreciated by the station master, but in between occasional 'differences' the passing scene was packed with interest. A warm summer evening in 1960, passengers recoiling as a 'Duchess' roars by with the down 'Caledonian' for Glasgow, or the sedate pace of Bescot's '2P' No 40646 wheeling the four-coach Birmingham portion of the CTAC 'Scottish Tours Express' southwards. There is just one serious challenge to the all steam atmosphere – the prototype English Electric 3,000hp *Deltic* diesel speeding south on the up 'Manxman' provokes much secret admiration. Survivors from another age and a very different tradition were the LNWR 0-8-0s, still quite common until 1962. It was amazing to see one of these veterans storming through at 50mph with an up express freight as late as 1961! Then there are the 'ones that got away': *Duchess of Montrose* on the Glasgow–Birmingham just weeks before the turn 'went diesel' – if only the photographer had remembered to remove the lens cap! – the ex-Crosti '9F' and Standard Caprotti '5' on the Snodland to Bay Horse cement, which just beat me to it, and the 'Britannia' on the 6.45am Euston–Windermere where I struggled into position just in time, but with my hot breath obliterating the viewfinder! Most recently, as *Duchess of Sutherland* went into the curve south of Winsford brilliantly lit, a brand new 'Pendolino' appeared on a down express and a snip of a shot of the two was missed.

Sometimes we would sit on the railway fence by Rilshaw Lane underbridge, listening intently for the block bells and crashing levers from nearby Winsford signalbox. Many autumn Saturday mornings found us there watching the endless stream of 'Black Fives' with

excursions for Blackpool Illuminations. Other memories include the release of pigeons from a 'Britannia'-hauled Liverpool–Crewe local, of Derby 'Patriot' No 45509 incredibly going north on a troop train of Southern stock in 1959, and 'Warship' diesel No D836, brand new on delivery from North British. On the down road, most firemen seemed to put on 'the first round' approaching Winsford – the smoke screens and associated aromas were memorable, especially that of the soft Welsh product sometimes used by Crewe North.

Minshull Vernon was the place to see trains in comfort, away from 'authority'. The platforms, closed in 1942, offered grandstand views of the action on the fast lines and close-ups of everything on the slow. So a Stanier Pacific working at speed with the down 'Midday Scot' could contrast with a 'Super D' waddling along the slow line, or pacing No 45512 *Bunsen* down the platform as she slowed for the Down Slow to Fast crossover with the 'Lakes Express'. Many expresses seemed to pass each other here, and a strategy to get both numbers was essential! It was a sad day when the platforms vanished with the 1962 electrification, but 'pilgrimages' continued until 1967. By then, the 'sparks effect' had truly arrived, but the 'Britannias' were still hammering through with the 1.46pm Barrow–Euston until March, and Stoke shed was sending its best 'Black Five', No 45350, on Blackpool excursions. Steam returned on summer Saturday extras, and the freight service was largely steam until the autumn. A final valedictory memory of July 1967: a sharp staccato audible for many minutes as the Stephenson link 'Black Five' No 44767 came south at 55mph with the 2.30pm Carlisle–Crewe Class 5 express freight.

The Liverpool electrification inaugurated from 1 January 1962 changed the whole character of the line – overhead wires, new stations and bridges, long welded rails, colour lights and 'hidden' communication systems. Most principal expresses were also diesel or electric hauled by 1962, although a substantial steam presence remained until 1967. A seismic moment was the mass withdrawal of all the remaining Stanier Pacifics in September 1964, and with the strains of 'Auld Lang Syne' saluting No 46256 as she came off the RCTS's 'Scottish Lowlander' special at Crewe, it really was the end of the old railway. Nobody doubted that such progress was essential – the performance and utilisation of the Class 86s after the electrification to London in April 1966 was simply revolutionary, incredibly better than anything that could regularly be achieved with steam. For my generation of enthusiasts, all this change came just a little too quickly, and it would have been nice to have had just a couple more years of the 'old regime'. No 46256 was just 16 years old when withdrawn, and alternative work for these machines and a more rational approach to modernisation with thorough testing of modern power, as in many developed European countries, could well have been fruitful.

Although educated in Winsford, it was some time before I realised what an interesting place the town had been as the main salt-producing centre in Cheshire. Not only was the Weaver Valley packed with salt works connected to both the CLC and LNWR branches into the town, but several obscure connections with unusual histories traversed Wharton Common linking the east bank salt works with the main line. The show was long over when in 1959 I first visited the Over & Wharton branch with its lines of Tilbury tanks and LNWR 0-8-0s awaiting scrapping. The rusting tracks and ramshackle buildings thereabouts added to the atmosphere of mystery and decay, and once a certain Stanier 2-8-0 had been secured for posterity, there was eventually time to research the history of 'Winsford Salt Sidings' contained herein.

This volume aims to recapture the atmosphere of the main line between Crewe and Warrington in the days of steam, with just an occasional glimpse of the machines that followed. This latter generation of modern traction – principally Classes 40, 47, 50, 81-87 and 90, has in turn now been superseded. The future lies in the hands of 'Voyagers' and 'Pendolinos', which will hopefully re-establish the 125mph West Coast main line in the forefront of British express performance as it was in 1966, and in the heyday of steam traction in the late 1930s. Just occasionally your author can be found with camera, padding along Clive Back Lane. The railway is busy with new-generation passenger trains and long-haul block freights, with the potential to make an even greater contribution to the nation's transport needs. It is still a captivating prospect, with the occasional appearance

of a Stanier Pacific providing a reminder of the days before the 'overheads' went up.

Please be my guests in enjoying that once so familiar prospect.

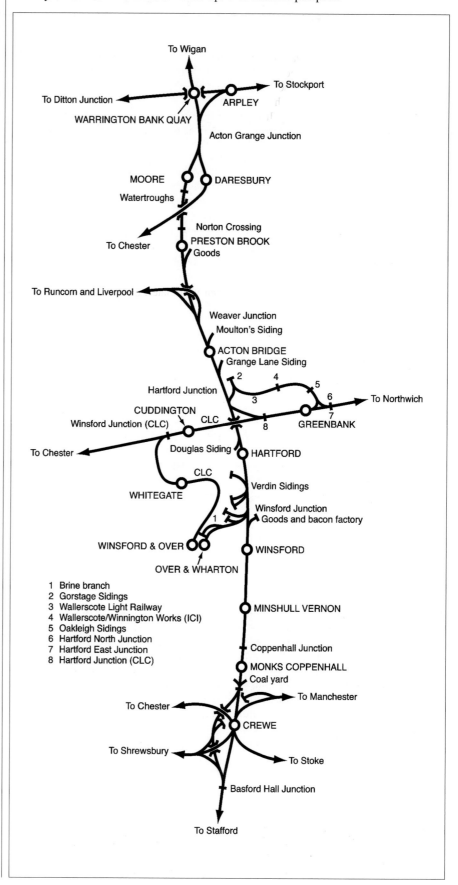

1 Brine branch
2 Gorstage Sidings
3 Wallerscote Light Railway
4 Wallerscote/Winnington Works (ICI)
5 Oakleigh Sidings
6 Hartford North Junction
7 Hartford East Junction
8 Hartford Junction (CLC)

1. CREWE: THE GREAT RAILWAY JUNCTION

Volumes have rightly been written about the West Coast route to Scotland, and this account aims simply to recreate something of the character and business of this great trunk route through Cheshire. It was frequently a line of epic performance, dictated by the presence of Crewe Works and the consequent need for trial running over the demanding Carlisle road, but above all it was a ceaselessly busy railway, dedicated to the trunk haul of passengers, freight and parcels. Linking London with Scotland via the conurbations of the West Midlands and North West, the line has been a vital transport artery for more than 165 years.

The Grand Junction Railway was promoted in 1833 to provide the North West with a rail connection to the south by linking the Liverpool & Manchester Railway at Newton, north of Warrington, with Birmingham. This city in turn was in the process of being linked to the capital by the London & Birmingham Railway, which opened in 1838. From the start the Grand Junction, which opened on 4 July 1837, was conceived as a direct trunk route. Planned by George Stephenson and constructed by Joseph Locke, it ignored intermediate settlements and took the most favourable line that topography would allow. So it struck boldly southwards from Warrington, striding across the incised meanders of the River Weaver on two impressively large viaducts, and tackling the undulations of the Cheshire Plain with substantial embankments and cuttings. It by-passed Runcorn, Northwich and Nantwich and skirted Winsford, heading for the gap in the main watershed of England created by the glacial overflow channel at Whitmore, thence via the Sow valley to Stafford and Birmingham. Ten miles north of Whitmore, the Sandbach-Nantwich turnpike crossed the line in the heart of verdant, open countryside. It was here that there was created in a mere 30 years or so perhaps the most famous railway junction, traffic centre and locomotive building establishment in the country. This was Crewe!

Initially the town developed as the junction of several routes to the south. Following the GJR came the Chester & Crewe Railway, opened on 1 October 1840 but already absorbed by the GJR and soon to provide the link to the two important ports of Birkenhead and Holyhead. After much protracted squabbling about misappropriation of GJR traffic and unsuccessful promotion of alternative routes to the south via the Trent Valley, the Manchester & Birmingham Railway followed on 10 August 1842. Four years later the GJR and M&B had become major constituents of the London & North Western Railway (LNWR), destined to become one of the most formidable joint stock companies in the country. All routes from Crewe were now part of the 'Premier Line', but this monopoly was broken when the North Staffordshire Railway arrived from Stoke-on-Trent on 9 October 1848. Ten years later, on 1 September 1858, the LNWR connected Crewe to Shrewsbury, and thence more importantly to its far-flung dominions in the Welsh Marches and South Wales. The alternative Great Western Railway (GWR) route from the West Midlands via Wellington and Market Drayton opened on 16 October 1867, preceded by the Cambrian Railways' line to Aberystwyth via Whitchurch on 27 July 1864. Finally came the LNWR branches from Sandbach to the Cheshire saltfield at Northwich on 11 November 1867, and from Whitchurch to Tattenhall Junction on 1 October 1872. Many of these lines were long-distance or regionally important routes with real traffic potential. Crewe was strategically placed to collect most traffic from the South East, Midlands and South West and to redistribute it towards the North West and Scotland, and across the Pennines to the North East.

But that was not all. Crewe was also conveniently placed at a mid-point between Liverpool/Manchester and Birmingham, and later strategically at the centre of the LNWR's far-flung empire stretching from Swansea and Holyhead in the south-west and west, Leeds and Carlisle in the east and north, and London in the south. And there was cheap agricultural land in abundance to facilitate the removal of the GJR's workshops from their cramped site at Edge Hill, Liverpool, in 1843. Within 20 years a locomotive-building and repair establishment had developed into a huge engineering manufactory that supplied the LNWR with virtually all its constructional and engineering requirements, expanding from the 'Old Works' site to a large, expansive position at the 'West End' of the town. By 1890 the Works had produced more than 3,000 locomotives, and the station was dealing with almost 1,000 trains per day.

As important as Crewe's role as a key passenger interchange was its role as a freight-handling centre, and in the days of traditional wagonload traffic a huge volume either traversed or was remarshalled at Crewe. All routes into Crewe carried major freight flows. From the south came the products of London and the West Midlands conurbations, heading for distribution throughout the North West and Scotland, as well as fruit and agricultural produce from the South East and export goods for the northern ports. Both routes from the Western Region brought much perishable traffic, manufactures from the West Midlands, and a wide range of imports from the South Wales ports. Coal traffic from this area was also considerable until the mid-1960s. The Chester line was always busy with port traffic from Holyhead and Birkenhead – agricultural products, cattle trains galore and general imports for national distribution, latterly chemicals and petroleum from south Merseyside. From the north came a wide range of manufactures, imports from Liverpool, and the trunk haul of manufactured items from the Scottish industrial belt. The Manchester line was fully occupied with trans-Pennine freight to Leeds and the North East, as well as salt and chemicals from Cheshire. From the Stoke line came heavy flows of coal to the North and North Wales, and merchandise to and from the East Midlands. All this traffic intermingled at and was redistributed from Crewe, where the activity in Basford Hall Yard was incessant throughout the day.

With the growth of traffic after 1880, the LNWR was under considerable pressure to enlarge the marshalling facilities at Crewe. The Stafford line was quadrupled in 1876 and, as part of the Crewe remodelling at the turn of the century, Basford Hall Yard was enlarged to a capacity of 2,350 wagons, the Down Yard, holding 1,600 wagons, being nearly twice the size that on the Up side. Further improvements came in the late 1920s when Gresty Lane Down Sidings opened and Basford Hall Up Sidings were lengthened and enlarged with six new roads. By the late 1930s the LMS claimed to be operating the 'busiest yard in Europe', dealing with 400 trains per day; 48,000 wagons per week from all over the country were detached at Crewe for re-marshalling into forward services. Each day more than 200 inward freights and trip workings detached some 7,000 wagons for remarshalling into a further 200 outward services at Basford Hall Sorting Sidings, North Stafford Sidings Up and Down, and Gresty Lane Up and Down sidings. Another 400 wagons of 'smalls' daily passed through the Tranship Shed to be marshalled into onward services. To handle such volumes of traffic, the Crewe Independent Lines were absolutely essential.

Up freights accessed the Independent Lines at Crewe Coal Yard on the North main line and at Sydney Bridge Junction on the Manchester line, then via tunnels under the North Junction to Salop Goods Junction where trains were regulated to Gresty Lane No 1 or to BH Sorting Sidings North, and thence to BH Up Sidings. Freight from Chester came from the North Junction via the Up Chester Independent line to Salop Goods Junction. Down freights from the south accessed the Independent Lines at Basford Hall Junction, then to Sorting Sidings South, Middle or North. Trains from Shrewsbury or the Western Region were regulated at Gresty Lane No 2 box to No 1 or 2 arrival lines, then to Gresty Lane Down Sidings. This group of sidings detached some 1,100 wagons daily, exchanging up to 400 wagons daily with Basford Hall across the Shrewsbury line at Gresty Lane No 1. Eastward services departed via the two through sidings at Gresty Lane No 1 to Salop Goods Junction for Liverpool, Manchester, the Eastern Region via Guide Bridge, Leeds, and Scotland via Carlisle.

North Stafford Up and Down Sidings handled traffic from the Potteries. Up trains had to travel via Crewe station then South Junction to exchange traffic in the NS Up Sidings. Down traffic was marshalled at NS Down Sidings, where it was sorted for forward services or tripped via the NS Cutting Spur to Basford Hall Down Sidings. The Sorting Sidings at Basford Hall comprised 50 roads set

Above:
Crewe North Junction, 19 July 1903
Two LNWR 'Alfred the Great' 4-4-0s, Nos 1965 *Charles H. Mason* and 1966 *Commonwealth*, in the charge of Crewe drivers Ben Robinson (of 1895 'Race to the North' fame) and Harland, get away with a Euston-Carlisle non-stop special composed mostly of luxurious 12-wheeled stock. The buildings of the Grease Works are just visible on the skyline, while the tail of a freight train emerges from the Down Liverpool Independent tunnel in the foreground. *LNWR Society 2278*

Left:
Crewe North Junction, Whit Saturday 1965
Viewed from an AM4 EMU on a local from Liverpool awaiting access to the former No 8 Bay, Class 5 No 45037 gets away vigorously with 1T67, the 09.46 Stoke–Blackpool excursion, typical of dozens that once ran from the West Midlands and the Potteries on peak weekends to North Wales and the Fylde coast. On the right, the Down Liverpool Independent Line climbs up from the freight underpass alongside the original GJR Erecting Shop of 1843. *A. Wilkinson*

between the running lines, with three reception lines between the up and down sides. The up side had 20 sidings with stop blocks, while the down had 30 double-ended sidings, accessed at either SS Middle or North. Trains marshalled at SS Middle departed from SS North to Shrewsbury via Gresty Lane or via Salop Goods Junction for other Down destinations.

Up freights were remarshalled at Basford Hall Up Sidings, having arrived via three reception lines or the Up Goods line. Some 1,500 wagons were also detached here daily for other destinations. Trains booked only for examination or locomotive purposes were dealt with at Sorting Sidings South, being regulated at SS North over the Up Fast Independent line, which was not signalled to SS Middle. All up freights from SS Middle and SS South then joined the Up Fast or Up Slow at Basford Hall Junction. Additionally, on peak holidays and Saturdays during the summer, up to 70 passenger trains from and to North Wales and the North were also routed via the Independent Lines.

Thus from the late 19th century Crewe's reputation as a locomotive stable, traffic centre and passenger interchange was probably unsurpassed. In 1950 the station was still handling some 400 trains per day (with almost as many freight trains being dealt with on the 'Independent Lines'). The railway was still overwhelmingly the town's major employer – 8,000 were employed in the Works alone, which performed some 40 locomotive overhauls per week in addition to new construction. In December 1958 Class 9F 2-10-0 No 92250 became the 7,337th (or 7357th – records differ) and last steam locomotive to be 'built at Crewe'. And what a lineage – Allen 2-2-2s and 2-4-0s, Ramsbottom's unique 2-2-2 *Cornwall* and 'DX' 0-6-0s, Webb's record-breaking 2-4-0 *Hardwicke* contrasted with his controversial Compounds, Whale's 'Precursors' and 'Experiments', the Bowen Cooke 'George Vs', 'Prince of Wales', 'Claughtons' and 'Super D' 0-8-0s, the outstandingly successful range of Stanier machines including the incomparable 'Duchesses', and the modern Ivatt and BR Standard types, to name only a few. Crewe survived to be the last British works to overhaul steam locomotives when, in February 1967, 'Britannia' Pacific No 70013 *Oliver Cromwell* became the last of some 125,000 steam overhauls undertaken over 124 years.

Not surprisingly, Crewe became an absolute Mecca for railway enthusiasts who crowded the station platforms, particularly in the 1950s and for much of the following decade. Well into the 1970s the station remained the absolute focal point of the London Midland Region, with vast amounts of passenger, parcels and freight traffic being handled. By this time, fundamental traction changes had taken place with the Euston–Manchester/Liverpool electrification inaugurated from 18 April 1966, the final closure of Crewe South depot to steam traction in November 1967, and the end of BR's use of steam traction from 4 August 1968. Although Crewe has since lost some of its importance due to changing traffic patterns and vastly different locomotive diagramming, with much more through working, it remains an absolutely key passenger junction and a significant freight centre.

Below:
Crewe North Junction, 9 July 1966
What a different perspective the 'overheads' make! This signalman's view from the North box shows 'Britannia' No 70010 *Owen Glendower* making a purposeful exit from Platform 2 with 1L27, the 11.40 Euston–Carlisle, through the complexities of what was still basically the 1906 layout. Electrification from London to the North West had been inaugurated from 18 April, and steam locomotives were becoming relatively scarce. *A. Wilkinson*

Above:
Crewe North Junction, 30 July 1965
Caught in almost the same position as the previous picture, one of Crewe South's best Class 5s, No 44680, gets away with 1S77, the *1pm* Crewe–Glasgow relief, running ahead of the down 'Royal Scot'. Note the Crewe Arms Hotel on the left. *A. Wilkinson*

2. THE GROWTH OF CREWE STATION AND ITS ENVIRONS

Initially facilities were very modest, consisting of a 'station house, an engine house and one spare engine', said *Osborne's Guide*. Nevertheless the station was designated 'First Class', enjoyed coach connections to Nantwich and Sandbach, and after 1840 could include the adjacent Crewe Arms Hotel among its facilities. The 'spare engine' was often needed to assist trains up the 1 in 177 gradient to Whitmore – the 'Up Hill Pilot' becoming very much a Crewe institution. The two-platform station was enlarged in 1840 with the opening of the Chester line, and included the M&B station in its 'detached' position when that line opened in 1842.

The opening of the Works in 1843, the formation of the LNWR in 1846 and the opening of the through route to Scotland in 1848 saw almost immediate further enhancement of the station. In 1842 it consisted of two platforms, 81 yards in length, together with facilities for horses and carriages and some small sidings. The platforms were extended in 1845/6, and

more track added. According to Sir F. Head, in *Stokers and Pokers*, 'Three pointsmen were constantly on duty, one of whom had 17 pairs of points to attend to.' By 1849 Crewe boasted 'a very handsome building in the Elizabethan style' (*Measome's Guide*, 1862). The platform awnings were remarkable, being supported on iron columns with the outer edge sweeping upwards in a concave curve, decorated with panels. Up and down through tracks had been added in the centre, and outwardly this was quite an imposing station, but its facilities were modest for a developing junction of six routes once the Shrewsbury line had opened in 1858.

During the 1860s a series of improvements were made in the course of which the basis of the eastern half of the present station (Platforms 3-6) emerged – two island platforms, lengthened south of the Nantwich road bridge, with two bays at the southern end and two bays at the end of the down platform. The main buildings on Platforms 4 and 5 date from 1867, and are

distinguished by the use of finely detailed buff and polychrome brickwork, careful window detail including the use of bays, and the 'Crewe greybeards', which are a feature of the keystones. The rather low, functional rather than inspiring trainsheds date also from this period, supported by plain iron columns featuring simple brackets and heavier cross girders creating a rather fragile but functionally graceful appearance. Many of the trainsheds were supported by distinctive sidewalls pierced by numerous round-headed openings and featuring decorative brickwork, with limited use of vertically glazed side screens at the south end of Platform 3.

To the west, the first of the North Shed buildings had appeared after 1850, but while a more spacious station had been created, there were still only two through tracks and little had been done to cope with increasing congestion on the railway. Between 1861 and 1876 the LNWR system grew by 600 route miles, with a further 20% increase by 1891. Train mileage increased by 30% in the same period. In

Right:

Crewe South steam shed, 5 May 1946
Operational from 1897 to 1967, this study of the north frontage closely reflects the November 1945 allocation of 124 freight locomotives. With standard LMS '3F' tanks and 0-6-0s for shunting, a predominance of 'Super D' 0-8-0s, and '5MTs' and '8Fs' for the heaviest and fastest jobs, 5B locomotives worked over every route from Crewe. With Crewe North shed, it was a major provider of power on the Warrington line, and the complex diagrams operated from LMS days also saw Camden, Edge Hill, Speke Junction, Warrington, Patricroft, Springs Branch, Preston, Carnforth, Carlisle and Polmadie locomotives, to name just a few, traversing the main line through Cheshire. *H. Townley, C. M. & J. M. Bentley collection*

1876 the line between Crewe and Stafford was quadrupled, and although two new platforms (Nos 3 and 6) were opened, little had been done to ease the bottleneck in the station area. By 1880 more than 200 trains per day were passing through Crewe.

Traffic growth in the 1880s led to serious congestion. The flat junctions at either end of the station, the shortage of platforms, and only one track in each direction for freight to avoid the station led to many delays and conflicting movements. In 1893 a comprehensive study of the problems found Crewe dealing with 1,000 trains per day, and recommended drastic changes.

Between 1896 and 1906 a wholesale and thoroughgoing programme of improvements to the station and track layout saw the creation of 46 miles of 'Goods Independent Lines', opened on 24 March 1901, from Basford Hall Junction in the south, alongside the newly developed Basford Hall Yards, then running in a cutting on the western side of the station before burrowing under the North Junction to join the Warrington and Manchester lines at Coal Yard and Sydney Bridge Junctions respectively. Spurs from Basford Hall to Gresty Lane No 1, and from Salop Goods Junction to Gresty Lane, connected with the Shrewsbury line, while the spur from Salop Goods Junction to Crewe North Junction provided for the Chester line. By this means it was possible to remove most of the freight traffic from the station area, although trains from Chester skirted the station to the west and those from the North Staffordshire line still had to proceed through the station. A later spur from North Staffordshire Sidings into Basford Hall Yard allowed indirect

diversion of southbound freights for the North Staffordshire route.

Integral with these improvements came the enlargement of Basford Hall Yards, the opening of Crewe South shed principally for around 130 freight, mixed-traffic and shunting locomotives, a new 147-vehicle carriage shed alongside the Stafford line just beyond the South Junction, and the provision of a Goods Transhipment Shed, 326 feet long and 188 feet wide, near Gresty Lane. Employing 500 men in two shifts, this very useful measure led to much more efficient wagon loading, and the shed could deal with 600 inward wagons per day, while another 500 were loaded with 20,000 outward packages. Finally, in 1906, a new island platform with fine buildings typical of the best LNWR stations, and featuring extensive trainsheds and vertically glazed draught screens, was added on the west side of the station (Platforms 1 and 2). With platforms over 1,500 feet long with 'scissors' crossovers at the halfway point and double bays inset at both ends, this almost doubled the capacity of the station.

In the 1920s the station consisted of six platforms and ten bays. The total length of the platforms was 3,790 yards, while four acres of the 4.75-acre station area were roofed over. By this time the area was handling up to 500 passenger and 200 goods trains daily, with up to 600-700 trains being dealt with in peak 24-hour periods on summer weekends. These were the facilities that served the station well through the traffic demands of two World Wars and the hectic post-war years. The LMS made some relatively minor improvements in 1938/9 when a single booking office and concourse on the

Nantwich Road bridge replaced individual booking offices on the platforms. By 1960 the station was still dealing with some 400 passenger and parcels trains per day.

How were these facilities typically used in steam days and before the 1985 re-organisation? Moving from west to east across the station, just outside the glass screens was No 1 Down Through Road, giving access to the Down Yard and to and from Platform 1 via the middle scissors crossover, and also providing a relatively little-used through route from South to North Junction. Then came Platforms 1 and 2, divided halfway by the scissors crossovers controlled by Crewe A and B boxes. To the east was the principal No 2 Down Through Road, separated from dual-direction No 3 Platform by the outer wall of the 1867 station with its distinctive rounded arches. Between Nos 4 and 5 Platforms was a long siding, followed by the Up Through Road. North of Nantwich Road bridge, and bridging the Up Through, was Scissors Crossing Box of 1876, which controlled the latterly rarely used scissor crossing on Platform 5 and closed on 17 November 1958. On the opposite side of this island was Platform 6, hard alongside the eastern retaining wall, reached by a somewhat cavernous approach between structures and set well south of the other platforms.

Platforms 1 and 2 were used for all the principal down services, and only when these were full was Platform 3 called upon. Platforms 3, 4 and 5 were used by up services, Platform 4 being the principal departure platform, while Platform 3 sometimes doubled as an Up Through Road in times of pressure. Platform 6 was used mainly by parcels services, many of which

Above:

Crewe station, south end, *c*1920

The complex layout of late LNWR days, typical of a major junction, largely remained until 1985. A semi-fast of very mixed composition waits to leave the Down Yard (left), while a 'Claughton' stands on No 1 Down Through Road waiting to return to the North shed. Another cluster of locomotives, including a 'Prince of Wales', stands by the North Stafford bays (right). Note the many headshunts and crossovers, designed for van traffic and multi-portioned trains and used to capacity until the 1970s. 'Never Ready Junction' it sometimes was, and as late as midnight on August Bank Holiday Friday 1965 all down platforms were occupied with trains standing on all approaches. Note the extensive awnings and trainsheds, much rationalised since the 1960s, and the main station administration building prominent between Platforms 1 and 2. *LNWR Society 712*

Left:

Crewe station, north end, 27 August 1965

This latter-day steam scene, with overhead wires and a 'Britannia' Pacific, has 'fresh off' No 70023 *Venus* taking hold of 1D43, the down day 'Irish Mail' for Holyhead, from bi-directional Platform 3. The shortened north footbridge leading to the North shed is on the right, with the new 1961 station concourse above the train. The line of arches marking the supporting wall to the overall roof above Platform 3 points to surviving parts of the late-1860s station. *A. Wilkinson*

originated or terminated in the Up Hill Sidings. This was particularly true of mid-mornings and overnight, while at other times the platform provided useful spare capacity for relief trains. No 5 Bay was usually the preserve of trains to and from Stoke and Derby, with No 6 or 'Western' Bay more usually used for parcels traffic, particularly overnight for the North and West Route. No 3 Bay and No 4 Bay were allocated to local services from the Wellington and Shrewsbury lines respectively, but could also deal with up to eight-coach trains if necessary. Nos 7 and 8 Bays were used for originating services to and from North Wales and for local services to Liverpool and semi-fasts to the North. No 9 Bay was the preserve of the infrequent motor trains to Northwich, while No 10 Bay dealt with locals to Manchester and could accommodate up to eight coaches. Nos 1 and 2 Bays accommodated arrivals from the Shrewsbury line, and other short trains, including the infrequent locals from Stafford and the midday semi-fast from Euston. They were, however, much more importantly used to accommodate parcels and perishable traffic, being fully occupied in this way from late afternoon until the following lunchtime.

3. 'THIS IS CREWE...': A DAY IN THE LIFE

'This is Crewe, Crewe station, Crewe.'

For most of the 20th century this was the standard introduction to train announcements. It was the prelude to meetings and partings, happy homecomings, the next stage of interminable or captivating journeys according to taste, and the harbinger of taut anticipation to the hundreds of enthusiasts who thronged the platforms in the 1950s.

'The train now approaching Platform 4 is the 09.10 hours from Liverpool Lime Street to Plymouth, going forward at 10.20 for Shrewsbury, Hereford, Pontypool Road, Bristol Temple Meads, Taunton, Exeter, Newton Abbot, Totnes and Plymouth. Restaurant Car and Buffet Car facilities are available on this service. The Kingswear portion will be attached at the rear, calling at Kingskerswell, Torre, Torquay, Paignton, Goodrington Sands, Churston and Kingswear. Change at Bristol for Weston-super-Mare and at Plymouth for principal stations to Penzance.'

Magic! It is 10.04am on a summer weekday in the early 1950s and Platform 4 is jammed with people, suitcases and barrows piled high with luggage and mailbags. On the Up Through Road the summer Manchester-Plymouth relief comes through behind Longsight Caprotti Class 5 No 44749. 'Plymouth, Bristol, Shrewsbury and Manchester London Road' read the carriage roof-boards. Then the trainsheds reverberate to the sound of ringing big ends and chonking anti-vacuum valves as 'the Plymouth' comes briskly to a stand behind Crewe North 'Black Five' No 44770 heading a mixed consist of 12 LMS and GWR coaches, with an LMS 12-wheeled Restaurant Car in the middle. Opposite, a Longsight '7P' 4-6-0 working to Pontypool Road is drawing to a stand in Platform 5 with the 9.30am Manchester-Swansea. Immediately, the 'Up Hill Pilot', '2P 4-4-0 No 40660, buffers up to the rear, making off with the Kingswear portion and attaching it to 'the Plymouth'. Simultaneously, Platform 3 is host to a Camden 'Scot' on the 8.00am Blackpool-Euston, and we have a grandstand view of her exertions as she gets away at 10.18. Whistles shrill down the platform, the signal aspect changes to green and at about 10.25 (all this is rarely accomplished by 10.20!) the guard brandishes his flag and we are off to the West Country. A glance backwards to Platform 3 reveals a Holyhead 'Scot' running in with the 7.30am Holyhead-Euston, on the left a couple of 'Jinties' are busy with parcels vans in the south bays, there will soon be the panorama of Crewe South shed to savour, and we might even get excited about the Shrewsbury or Newton Abbot 'Castle' that will come on at Shrewsbury...

So ends a 20-minute microcosm of activities at Crewe – a scene repeated numerous times on weekdays (less so on Saturdays) as trains exchanged portions, vans and locomotives.

Let us therefore go back and try to recreate the hectic atmosphere of a summer Saturday in the early 1950s. BR is operating a 'social' railway, struggling to satisfy demand regardless of cost. Car ownership is still very limited, air travel confined to a privileged minority, and many trains that run as portions in the week translate into Saturday reliefs and excursions galore. Perhaps three-quarters of the services change engines, while extra coaches are found and added as required. The same applies to vans of parcels, sausages, fruit or bananas, not forgetting the milk tanks that are found swinging along on convenient expresses. DMUs are as yet unheard of, so local services need marshalling and fresh locomotives. Crewe is a major parcels centre and the platforms are never free of trolleys, parcels and mailbags since most principal expresses carry mail throughout the day. The platforms are abuzz with people – passengers with luggage, porters with barrows, enginemen with their distinctive overalls and 'snap' baskets, harassed Platform Foremen... And if you think all this is hectic, don't forget the freight over on the Independent Lines. It is only a little quieter than on weekdays, as the freights whistling for the 'muckhole' tunnels under the North Junction constantly remind us.

Let's 'book on' with the Friday night shift at 10pm. The two hours to midnight are the quietest of the day with just 24 trains, but by no means uninteresting. On the down side, the overnight Anglo-Scottish mail and sleepers and their connections begin to arrive. The 8.20pm Birmingham–Chester and 6.55pm Hereford–Crewe parcels appear in Platform 1 and No 1 Through Road between 10.06 and 10.15, while the 7.15pm Euston-Lairg newspapers/mail pauses on the Down Through at 10.13 behind a Crewe North '5XP'. Over on Platforms 1 and 2, lifts are whirring and trolleys stacked with mail are being marshalled as passengers resignedly await the Scottish overnights. Behind the draught screens at the north end of Platform 1 a Crewe North 'Duchess' is waiting for the 'First Perth', which rolls in at 10.21pm behind a Camden Pacific. The 1.35pm parcels from Broad Street is close behind on No 1 Through, and sets back noisily into the Down Sidings. There is even a 10.50 Crewe-Perth relief of eight coaches sitting in No 8 Bay behind a rather weary Crewe 'Patriot', No 45511 *Isle of Man*. Another 'Duchess' is backing down from the North shed into No 9 Bay for the 'Second Perth', which uses Platform 3 from 10.56 to 11.10pm. We savour the prospect of these two magnificent beasts, tenders piled with coal and safety valves simmering, moving off with their heavy trains for the 292-mile lodging turns to Perth (some of us would give our right arms to be on their footplates!).

Next into Platform 2 is the WR 'North Mail', the 12.00pm Penzance–Liverpool, headed by a Shrewsbury Class 5, which spends the next hour shunting and exchanging mail. The 6.30pm Swansea–York follows in Platform 1 North from 11.27 to 12.01, with the 10.10pm Birmingham–Crewe behind in No 1 South. Mailbags are flying out of trains onto trolleys to be tripped down to Platform 2 South where the 'Down Special TPO', the 8.30pm Euston to Glasgow, is due from 11.44 to 11.58. Two Crewe North Pacifics exchange places, a whistle shrills, a green light from the rear and the 'Princess' Pacific, exhaust reverberating from the trainsheds, takes the 'West Coast Postal' through the scissors crossover heading for Scotland with all the majesty and mystery implied in Auden's famous lines 'This is the Night Mail crossing the Border...' Almost unseen, a Holyhead 'Royal Scot' sneaks by on No 1 Through Road with the 8.45pm Euston–Holyhead. Meanwhile, on the up side, matters are much quieter, with just a few terminating locals and one express – the 7.35pm Holyhead–Birmingham, which stands in Platform 3 from 11.35 to 12.40am to connect with both down and up Special TPOs.

It may be the middle of the night, but there are 68 trains to deal with over the next four hours. First is the York mail, which leaves Platform 1 at 12.01am. Hard behind is the down 'Irish Mail', the 8.52pm Euston–Holyhead, which arrives at 12.02 behind a Holyhead 'Royal Scot'. Two Scottish services follow – the 9.10pm Euston–Glasgow on the Down Through behind an Upperby Pacific, and the 9.17pm Euston–Glasgow St Enoch follows at 12.23am. Meanwhile a Preston Class 5 leaves from the Down Yard with the 12.15 Preston parcels, going slow line to Minshull Vernon. The 10.55pm from Wellington – a '57xx' Pannier and 'B' set – fusses into No 2 Bay, followed by an Aston '5XP', which rolls down Platform 2 at 12.26am with the 11.05pm Birmingham–Glasgow Buchanan Street, while the 'North Mail' is away from No 8 Bay for Liverpool at 12.25. The 11.05pm Birmingham–Glasgow occupies Platform 1 from 12.48 to 1.05am, exchanging its Crewe unrebuilt 'Scot' for a 'Princess' Pacific from the same stable. Platform 2

simultaneously deals with the 9.25pm Euston–Glasgow sleeper, headed by an Upperby Pacific. Two express freights – the 8.50pm Nottingham–Edge Hill and 8.50pm Camden–Carnforth – quickly occupy the Down Through, while Platform 2 deals with the 10.45pm Euston–Manchester sleeper and its preceding relief, and it is coming up to 1.55am as the 10.50pm Euston-Perth rolls to a stop in Platform 2 to exchange its Camden 'Duchess' for a sister from Crewe North.

Matters are even busier on the up side, where the focus is initially on the mail interchange with the 'Up Special TPO', the 6.35pm from Glasgow, which occupies Platform 4 from 12.25 to 12.37am. Just ahead is the 9.30pm Windermere–Euston, which is in Platform 5 from 12.03 to 12.25, after which come three 'overnight endurance tests' to the West Country. The 11.15pm Manchester Victoria–Paignton is dealt with on the Up Through Road, while the 11.35 Liverpool–Penzance is exiled to Platform 6 from 12.21 to 12.48am, followed by the 12.35am Manchester–Penzance from 1.25 to 2.00am. Platform 3 is busy with overnight mail and (nominally) passenger services – the 10.20pm Leeds–Crewe and 9.50pm York–Swansea – between 12.57 and 2.15am, Stanier 'Black Fives' from a variety of sheds being prominent on these services.

The first up Anglo-Scottish overnight is the 5.40pm Glasgow–Euston, which uses No 5 Platform from 12.41 to 1.10am, exchanging Crewe North Pacifics. The up Liverpool sleeper follows from 1.13 to 1.22am, probably headed by an Edge Hill 'Royal Scot'. Platform 4 then plays host to the 1.25am to Cardiff, followed by the terminating 6.30pm parcels from Holyhead. Platform 5 then accommodates the Law Junction–Broad Street meat from 1.42 to 2.15am, while the Carlisle–Birmingham fish pauses on the Up Through from 1.47 to 2.45, exchanging Upperby and Crewe North Class 5s. This has been a very busy hour or so; a succession of trains, bleary-eyed passengers mixing with busy platform staff, West Country holidaymakers struggling with luggage to the outer extremes of Platform 6, mail everywhere, and the station lifts very busy. Quite a pageant of motive power, too.

The steady pace continues, with 34 trains to process in the next two hours. Shortly after 2.00am on the down side trains leave from Platform 1 North and 2 South for Holyhead, Liverpool and Manchester. The medium-distance

overnights now appear, the 11.15pm Euston–Blackpool North being overtaken by the 11.05pm Euston–Windermere by use of the scissors crossover on Platform 2 between 2.13 and 2.18am, while the 11.25pm Euston–Holyhead uses Platform 3 from 2.28 to 2.36. All change engines at Crewe and, if power is tight, a 'Patriot' may well be turned out for the Holyhead or Windermere, a Carnforth '5XP' being booked for the Blackpool. The 11.00pm Euston–Glasgow sleeper comes by on the Down Through at 2.51am behind a Camden 'Duchess', after which a brace of parcels trains – Euston–Carlisle, Marylebone–Preston and Willesden–Carlisle – are accommodated at Platforms 2 and 1 North between 2.51 and 4.45am.

The 4.40pm Penzance–Manchester pauses in No 2 Platform from 3.41 to 3.54am, and the 12.40am Euston–Glasgow passes on the Down Through, before No 2 Platform is again needed for the 12.50am Euston–Holyhead from 3.56 to 4.04am. On the up road, matters are quieter and there is time to work Edge Hill–Stoke and Birkenhead–Beeston freights through the station. The 2.00am Stockport–Bristol parcels occupies Platform 6 from 2.45 to 4.03am, while the 2.50am Stoke Papers starts from 5B, delivering the 'early editions' as it passes the South Box. The up 'Irish Mail' in charge of a Holyhead '7P' and men calls at Platform 3 from 3.05 to 3.15am, followed by a breathless Alsager '4F' on the midnight Class F from Chester to Alsager, closely pursued by the 1.10am Holyhead–Euston, due in Platform 3 at 3.20am. As dawn breaks more Anglo-Scottish services appear, the 9.25pm from Glasgow exchanges Upperby and Crewe Pacifics in Platform 4 from 3.32 to 3.37am, followed by the 8.15pm from Perth from 3.40 to 4.00am to change Crewe '8Ps'. The 10.50pm from Glasgow goes through at 3.50am behind an Upperby '7P' or '8P' – altogether a very pleasant nocturnal interlude for admirers of Stanier Pacifics!

Just 25 trains to handle in the next two hours – almost the quietest of the day. The 2.15am Bescot–Garstang Class D rolls by on the Down Through shortly after 4.00am, and the 2.00pm Penzance–Crewe parcels terminates in No 1 South. Close behind at 4.10am is the 12.05am Cardiff–Liverpool, to spend 70 minutes reposing in No 1 South. A Crewe South '4F' with a Middlewich crew leaves No 7 Bay with the single-van 4.56am Northwich parcels. Locals to Manchester, Chester, Morecambe and Warrington leave between 5.15 and 6.00am, the 5.15pm Bescot–Carlisle Class

E passes on the Down Through, and the 12.02am from Euston terminates in Platform 3. The up side is much busier; Platform 3 accommodates the 1.45am Holyhead–Euston from 4.01 to 4.11am, the 5.15pm from Inverness exchanges Crewe Pacifics in Platform 4 from 4.42 to 4.52am, before the 11.15pm Glasgow–Birmingham exchanges a Crewe '8P' for an unrebuilt 'Scot'. The following Edinburgh–Birmingham swaps Upperby and Crewe '5X' 4-6-0s in Platform 4 from 5.14 to 5.30am. Two freights are then rapidly processed – the 3.20am Ellesmere Port–Crewe Class H at 5.30 behind a 'Super D', and the 3.30am Speke Junction–Alsager Class F with another Alsager '4F', both heading for North Stafford Sidings. Finally the 5.40am to Birmingham moves quietly out of No 4 Bay behind a Monument Lane 'Compound'.

As the day shift books on, relative peace reigns for a couple of hours before the real pressures of the day begin. An Alsager '4F' goes by on the Down Through with the 5.30am Alsager–Hooton Class F, while No 41229 heads the Northwich motor out of No 9 Bay at 6.15am. Then there is only the 1.10am Marylebone–Crewe parcels terminating on the Down Through at 6.54am. A '2P' in the charge of Whitchurch men brings the 6.54am from that point into No 2 North at 7.16am, the 7.23 local to Manchester leaves Platform 1 behind a Stanier 2-6-4 tank, and the 3.00am Marylebone parcels terminates at 7.32am, 'Jinties' busying themselves shunting the vans from both parcels services. The Northwich 'Dodger' departs again at 7.32, paralleling the '2P', which is off to Chester, followed by a Class 5 with the 7.42am local to Liverpool. A WR 'Hall' delivers

the 9.45pm parcels from Eastleigh on No 1 Down Through at 7.45am, and locals to Chester and Manchester depart at 7.48 and 7.50, just before the 6.20am Birmingham–Liverpool is into Platform 2 at 7.53.

Much the same pattern of occasional freight and local passengers applies on the up side. The 6.05am to Wellington is followed on the Up Through by the 4.15am Stott Lane–Bushbury Class H exchanging a Patricroft 'Super D' for a Crewe '8F', then the 5.40am Longsight–Crewe empty coaching stock (ECS) bound for the carriage shed, and the 5.15am Edge Hill–Sudbury Junction Class E, which exchanges Crewe and Willesden Class 5s. A whole series of locals to and from Crewe occupies the half-hour from 7.00am, culminating in the arrival of the 5.30am from Preston in Platform 5 at 7.35. The 12.01am Glasgow–Willesden parcels is into Platform 6 at 7.43, exchanging Crewe Class 5s and departing behind the 7.50am Euston, which leaves Platform 3 behind a Camden '5X'. The 4.28 Carlisle fish terminates in Platform 6 at 7.55.

On the north footbridge the first hardy observers arrive, with 38 trains booked in the next two hours. Boat trains, business expresses and heavy traffic for Birmingham and the West Country feature on the up side, while on the down a never-ending stream of regular trains, reliefs and excursions heads for the North and North Wales with hardly any let-up until mid-afternoon. The parade starts with a brace of Class 5s on the 6.25am Birmingham–Blackpool North, 6.52am Walsall–Llandudno and 7.00am Cheadle–Llandudno on the Down Through, with a pressured Alsager '4F' on the 8.05am Alsager-Hooton Class F at 8.30. The

8.10am Stoke–Liverpool in Platform 2 is overtaken by the 6.20am Nottingham–Llandudno on the Down Through, while the 7.00am Birmingham–Manchester does business at Platform 1 from 8.50, connecting with the 9.05 Bangor and 9.10 Liverpool in the North Bays. There is plenty for supporters of Class 5s, 'Jubilees' and 'Patriots' in this little session, with the odd '5MT' 2-6-0 if power is tight. Platform 1 now hosts the 9.20am Holyhead, while the time-honoured 9.25am Perth is rolling into No 2 South from the carriage shed behind a Polmadie 'Scot', possibly No 46121 *Highland Light Infantry, City of Glasgow Regiment*. The rush to the coast continues: Stechford–Llandudno, Crewe–Blackpool and Stoke–Blackpool North trains are rapidly processed in Platforms 1 and 2, with the 8.20am Birmingham–Liverpool in No 2 from 9.45 to 9.56.

On the up side, Platform 5 hosts the up 'Ulster Express', the 6.30am Heysham–Euston, from 8.31 to 8.42, exchanging a Carnforth '5X' for a Camden '7P'. The 6.30am Morecambe terminates in Platform 5 immediately afterwards. Platform 3 accommodates the 6.30am Llandudno–Euston at 8.45, a Chester Class 5 giving way to a Crewe '5X'. There is now no let-up on the up main platforms – the 8.00am Liverpool–Coventry in No 4 from 9.02 to 9.10, the 8.10am Manchester–Penzance in No 5 from 9.06 to 9.15, the 8.20am Liverpool–Euston in No 3 from 9.10 to 9.18, the 8.50am Liverpool–Penzance on the Up Through at 9.36, and the 8.20am Preston–Bristol in No 3 between 9.48 and 10.00. Another ten up local and ECS services have been accommodated as well.

Another 38 trains have to be handled before midday. The down side sees the

Right:
Crewe station, south end, 16 June 1951
A typically busy scene captured from Platform 2.
Ian Allan Library

Left:
Crewe, Platform 4, 9 September 1950
In a panorama from the eastern half of the north footbridge, 'Duchess' No 46250 *City of Lichfield* (note the well-emptied tender) runs in with a southbound express – probably the Glasgow–Birmingham day service. The usual enthusiast 'congregation' is at the north end of the platform (and beyond!).
B. W. L. Brooksbank, Initial Photographics

8.38am Walsall–Blackpool North, 9.45am Stoke–Blackpool North, 8.50am Derby–Llandudno and 9.15am Birmingham–Liverpool between 10.05 and 10.52, while the 8.25am Coventry–Blackpool goes by on the Down Through at 10.30. Wherever would the railway be without Stanier's 'Black Fives'? The 11.00am relief to Workington is ready in No 8 Bay, alongside the 11.00am Llandudno, the latter with a 2-6-4 tank if power is short. The 6.40am Euston–Windermere comes into No 1 South laden as always with additional parcels vans. The 8.00am Euston–Holyhead comes around the Windermere on No 1 Through Road, accessing Platform 1 North via the scissors crossover. The 'Scot' on the Windermere gets away at 11.14am, using the crossover and disappearing behind the draught screens to get round the Holyhead, whose '7P' is taking water before leaving at 11.25. Platform 2 is then host to the 'crack' 8.30am Euston–Liverpool, which pauses between 11.44 and 11.50 in charge of a good Edge Hill 'Duchess'.

Across the station the 9.15am Manchester-Paignton goes by on the Up Through at 10.06, and a Camden '7P' runs into Platform 3 with the 8.00am Blackpool–Euston. The 9.25am Manchester–Swansea is into Platform 5 at 10.15, with the 9.15am Liverpool–Plymouth halting simultaneously in No 4. The up 'Mancunian' follows, the chirruping three-cylinder beat of its Longsight 'Scot' reverberating through the trainsheds as she gets the road for the climb to Whitmore. Engines change in Platform 3, a Chester Class 5 giving way to a Camden '7P' on the 7.30am Holyhead–Euston. An Edge Hill '5X' traverses the Up

Through with the 10.10am Liverpool–Euston, while Platform 3 accommodates the 8.55am Llandudno–Euston from 10.50 to 10.55. Two Manchester and Liverpool to Birmingham services are rapidly dealt with at Platform 4 from 10.57 to 11.12am. The 'congregation' at the north end of Platform 4 gives a rapturous welcome to Edge Hill's No 46207 *Princess Arthur of Connaught* as she majestically strides along the Up Through with the 16-coach 'Merseyside Express', spot on time at 10.55am. Yet another Llandudno-Euston rolls into Platform 3 from 11.06 to 11.28, exchanging Holyhead and Crewe '7Ps'. Meanwhile, the Up Through hosts the 9.15am Blackpool North-Cardiff, the 10.30am Liverpool-Walsall leaves from Platform 4, and attention turns to the Crewe 'Compound' on the 11.20am Derby in No 6 Bay.

There are no fewer than 49 trains to deal with in the next two hours. Platforms are awash with passengers and luggage, and there is full attendance at all the enthusiast vantage points around the station. The north footbridge is jam-packed tight, give or take the odd loco-crew and even the occasional passenger! On the down side, the 12.08pm Blackpool and 12.10pm Manchester stand adjacent in the North Bays, and the 12.18pm Liverpool is ready to go in No 1 North. The 7.38am Cardiff–Manchester headed by a Shrewsbury Class 5 occupies Platform 2 from 12.19 to 12.22, and the 9.20am Euston–Llandudno follows into Platform 1. The 9.35am Euston–Manchester passes at 12.30 on the Down Through with a Longsight 'Scot'. Platform 1 is then busy with the 8.55am Cardiff–Manchester and 8.15am Bristol–Liverpool between 12.33 and 12.45, connecting into

the 11.15am Birmingham–Glasgow in Platform 2 from 12.40 to 1.00, exchanging a Crewe unrebuilt 'Scot' for Polmadie's No 46231 *Duchess of Atholl*. All eyes turn to the Down Through as the 'Royal Scot', recently equipped with a new set of BR standard coaches in carmine and cream livery, passes behind an Upperby 'Duchess' in the charge of Polmadie men.

Two Stanier 2-6-4 tanks head the 1.00pm Chester and 1.01pm Manchester out of No 1 North and No 7 Bay, but more interesting is the Upperby 'Jubilee' backing on to the 11.25am Birmingham–Glasgow in Platform 2, and the 10.08am Euston–Glasgow exchanging Camden and Crewe Pacifics in Platform 1. Soon afterwards an Upperby 'Scot' rolls into Platform 2 with the 10.20am Euston–Perth, and the passage of the 10.30am Euston–Liverpool at 1.28 behind an Edge Hill 'Princess' completes this pageant of premier LM steam power. The 12.15pm from Wellington arrives in No 3 Bay behind a '51xx' tank, followed by the 12.10pm Birmingham–Manchester in Platform 1 between 1.36 and 1.43. A Camden 'Scot' heads past on the Down Through with the 10.48am Euston–Blackpool at 1.50, while the 10.30am Euston–Carlisle is in Platform 2 exchanging Rugby and Preston '5Xs'. Over in No 7 Bay one of Crewe's few remaining 'Compounds' may get a run out on the 1.58pm Llandudno, while the early turn men, now on their knees, are relieved by their late-shift colleagues.

Matters are equally busy on the up road, evidenced by the number of times Platform 6 has to be used. The 9.45am Blackpool Central–Euston halts in No 3 from 12.07 to 12.09, followed by the

Right:
Crewe, Platform 2, 29 June 1952
The down 'Royal Scot' arrives from the south, rolling down Platform 2, the principal northbound departure platform, behind a machine of definite quality – Camden's 'Coronation' class 4-6-2 No 46237 *City of Bristol. E. R. Morten, courtesy of J. R. Morten*

9.45am Blackpool North–Bletchley in Platform 4, and somehow the 10.15am Llandudno–Derby goes right across the layout to call at Platform 6 between 12.04 and 12.06. The 6.35am Workington–Euston is in No 4 from 12.12 to 12.25, while the 8.05am Carlisle–Birmingham pauses in Platform 3 from 12.23 to 12.32. The long-established 8.20am Carlisle–Euston occupies No 3 Platform from 12.51 to 1.00, probably picking up a couple of vans while its exchange of Camden '7Ps' breaks the monotony of Class 5s (albeit from a variety of depots) on up services. A Mold Junction Stanier 2-6-0 on a Chester diagram rests in Platform 5 from 12.33 to 12.40pm with the 11.05am Rhyl–Stoke, while a Holyhead Class 5 and a borrowed Crewe South 'Crab' exchange places on the 8.50am Penychain–Stoke in Platform 6 from 12.43.

Next comes the 11.55am Manchester–Plymouth in Platform 4 at 12.55 behind a Longsight 5X, the 11.40am Liverpool–Rugby slow in No 5 from 12.59 to 1.11, leaving Platform 3 for the 12 midday Manchester–Cardiff, which sports a Longsight Caprotti 5. The 10.55am from Blackpool North terminates in Platform 6 at 1.09 and the 12.27pm Chester is into No 10 Bay at 1.13, while Crewe's sole Fowler 2-6-4 tank, No 42318, leaves No 6 Bay with the 1.35pm to Derby. The 9.55am Portmadoc–Euston 'Welshman' occupies the Up Through at 1.43 behind a Rugby '5X', and a Preston '5X' rolls into Platform 4 at 1.53 with the up 'Lakes Express', followed by the 'Horse and Cart', the 7.50am Holyhead–Crewe parcels, terminating in Platform 5 at 1.58pm before setting back into the Up Hill Sidings. Anything can turn up on this: Polmadie's

No 46222 *Queen Mary*, 'fresh off', pleases the Platform 4 cognoscenti no end!

The hectic pace continues with 44 trains booked over the next two hours. On the down side Platform 2 copes with the 11.50am Bletchley and 10.55am Euston–Blackpool, both changing engines, the latter from a Camden '7P' to a Kingmoor '5X'. Hidden behind the draught screens on No 1 Through Road, the 11.15am Euston–Portmadoc smartly exchanges Edge Hill and Chester '5Xs' between 2.30 and 2.34pm. The 11.22am Euston–Llandudno follows with a Crewe '7P'. Yet another Llandudno leaves No 7 Bay at 2.45pm, and there's even a Chester local at 2.50! In Platform 2 the 11.45am Euston–Manchester arrives at 2.51 behind a Longsight 'Scot', while the 11.52am Euston–Workington follows on the Down Through with a Preston '5X'. Next, the

Right:
Crewe North Junction, Summer 1956
Unnamed rebuilt 'Patriot' No 45528 (later *REME*) swings off the Chester line and heads for Platform 3 with the heavily loaded up 'Welshman', the 11.00am Portmadoc-Euston, against the familiar backdrop of (from the left) North shed, the Chester line, Old Works, North signalbox, north main line, Manchester line, Grease Works and Up Hill Sidings. Strangely, most of the enthusiast 'congregation' appears to be on holiday. *Martin Welch*

Above:
Crewe North shed, *c*1910
A definite highlight was always the breathtaking panorama across the front of the North shed, invariably featuring premier steam passenger power in profusion, represented here by a 'Precursor' 4-4-0 and several 'Experiment' 4-6-0s together with Webb 2-4-0s and a 'Cauliflower' 0-6-0 for secondary services. Operational from *c*1850 to 1965, it typically had an allocation of more than 120 locomotives, and by LMS days its engines and men ranged widely from London to Glasgow and Perth and associated lines. The route knowledge of the 'Top Link' men was truly formidable, and many record runs on the West Coast route were the work of Crewe enginemen. *C. M. & J. M. Bentley collection*

10.25am Swansea–Manchester Mayfield via Central Wales occupies Platform 2 North from 3.00 to 3.09pm, to be followed by the 12.05pm Euston-Liverpool in No 2 South from 3.05 to 3.10, and the 11.58am Euston–Workington is in Platform 1 from 3.04 to 3.12 exchanging Camden and Preston '5Xs'. The 1.30pm Birmingham–Blackpool North halts on the Down Through for 10 minutes from 3.07pm, exchanging Aston and Kingmoor Class 5s. The 1.45pm Birmingham–Manchester follows immediately into Platform 2 from 3.16 to 3.20, and there's another 1.55pm from Birmingham due in at 3.22! A '2P' heads the 'Calveley Milk' out of the Down Sidings at 3.35pm, and the 8.10am Paignton–Manchester is booked to pass on No 1 Through at 3.42 (some hope – this *is* a summer Saturday!), while Platform 1 deals with the 11.00am Aberystwyth–Manchester. Hopefully the 9.25am Bournemouth–Liverpool is into Platform 2 at 3.47pm, but how much time has it lost in the struggle over the S&D and through congested Birmingham? The train is booked to split into Liverpool and Manchester

portions, and must clear Platform 2 before the afternoon Scottish services appear.

Mid-afternoon finds the up side equally busy. A Camden '7P' on the 12.15pm Blackpool Central-Euston runs into Platform 3 at 2.00pm. The Northwich motor and a Liverpool local sneak in, the latter into Platform 6, followed by the 12.15pm Blackpool–Birmingham and locals from Manchester and Chester, the latter with milk tanks from Calveley. Crewe 'Patriot' No 45507 *Royal Tank Corps* is wuffling out of the Up Hill Sidings and through Platform 6 with the 2.37pm Pontypool Road parcels. Room has now to be found for the 1.15pm Edge Hill–Willesden Class D headed by Crewe's No 44680 to change crews between 2.40 and 2.46 – Platform 6 is a possibility. A roar goes up from the masses at the north end, as an Edge Hill 'Princess' comes by on the Up Through with the 2.10pm Lime Street-Euston at 2.45. Five minutes later, the 12.55pm Llandudno–Nottingham traverses the layout to access Platform 6. A brief lull allows the forward engine for the 9.30am Glasgow–Birmingham – the

pioneer unrebuilt 'Scot' No 46100 – to be got off the North shed, just one of a constant stream of light engine movements to and from the depot throughout the day.

Missing on a Saturday are the trains of engines going to and from the Works, the occasional appearance of a venerable Works shunter, and those locomotives 'fresh off' the Works going for running-in trips to Whitmore or Shrewsbury, not forgetting the 'Rag Mail' of stores vans from the Works, whose regular incumbent Webb 2-4-2 tank No 46680 can be seen reposing alongside the North shed. Intense excitement surrounds the debate over what is currently halted at the North Junction home signals. 'Semi!' goes the cry of identification, followed by whoops of delight as Polmadie's immaculate No 46232 *Duchess of Montrose* – the subject of a recent Hornby model – rolls in with the 16-coach Glasgow-Birmingham at 2.55pm. Thirteen minutes later, the crowds are again in ecstasy as another equally smart Polmadie beauty, No 46230 *Duchess of Buccleuch*, heads the up 'Royal Scot', very much the highlight of the afternoon.

Above:
Crewe, Platform 1, 1956
The north footbridge provided a wonderful panorama of the North Junction until it disappeared in 1958. The impressive lines of 'Duchess' Pacific No 46239 *City of Chester* are unmistakable as she sets off with a northbound express. The North shed is on the left, the Old Works buildings in the centre, and the newly repainted North Junction power box of 1940 on the right. *Martin Welch*

Right:
Crewe North Junction, Whit Saturday 1965
A rearward view as No 45037 heads towards Crewe Coal Yard. The Old Works buildings in the background became the main LMS Boiler Shop in 1925 (the riveting tower is prominent on the left), closing finally in 1965/6. Alas, an excellent proposal to convert the buildings into a railway museum failed in 1969/70, and they were demolished by 1976 to accommodate a relief road and supermarket – a disaster for the town's rich railway heritage. *A. Wilkinson*

Close behind is the 10.12am Edinburgh–Birmingham, 12 coaches trailing two six-wheeled milk tanks from Carlisle behind Crewe's No 45543 *Home Guard* piloted by No 40659.

Another six-beater exhaust announces the arrival in Platform 3 at 3.21pm of the 1.05pm Llandudno–Euston, with Crewe's No 45689 *Ajax*, a name in later years locally famous as the 'foaming cleanser' of TV advertisement fame. Then the 1.20pm Llandudno–Derby appropriately comes across to Platform 6 behind a 'Compound'. At the south end a '51xx' tank heads the 3.15pm Wellington from No 3 Bay, followed from No 4 Bay by the 3.28pm Salop local made up of the locomotive, stock and tanks from the 2.00pm from Chester. Further roars from the north end announce the arrival of a Camden 'Duchess' with the 10.06am Glasgow–

Euston – into 4 Platform at 3.32pm – the subsequent arrival of two 'Black Fives' with the 1.55pm Blackpool–Stoke and 1.40pm Llandudno–Derby being very small beer.

It is now almost 4.00pm with no fewer than 51 trains booked over the next two hours. In the down direction Anglo-Scottish services mix with erratically running trains from the West Country, threatening planned platform occupation and causing delays. The north footbridge is positively heaving with youthful (and not so youthful!) humanity, avidly intent on watching the drama unfold. The 1.05pm Euston–Glasgow comes down No 2 Platform at 4.07pm behind an Upperby '7P', while a 'Crab' appears in Platform 1 with the 8.55am Paignton–Manchester instead of the booked Class 5. Feverish anticipation on the north footbridge greets the arrival of the down 'Midday Scot' behind Crewe's No 46212 *Duchess of Kent*, with No 46227 *Duchess of Devonshire* of Polmadie waiting to take over – this is the place to see the 'big uns'! At 4.19pm the guard's whistle shrills and there is no mistaking the captivating deep but sharp beat of the 'Duchess' as she takes hold of the 16-coach train and strides majestically across the layout to disappear behind the North box, her quickening exhaust rhythmically echoing from the buildings of the Old Works – an unforgettable experience worth coming miles to see!

With such a prospect, little attention is given to the 11.15am Swansea–Manchester exchanging Crewe Class 5s in Platform 1, the 4.30pm Northwich motor setting out of No 9 Bay, or the Chester 2-6-4 tank on the 4.26pm Bangor in No 7 Bay. Following into No 2 Platform is the 1.30pm Euston-Blackpool, preceded by a relief that starts from Platform 2 at 4.33pm, both headed by Kingmoor locomotives, with probably a '5XP' on the Euston service. As 5.00pm nears, the 10.05am Exeter–Manchester and 8.45am Plymouth–Liverpool keep matters busy in Platforms 1 and 2. The Liverpool exchanges Shrewsbury and Crewe Class 5s, but the Manchester has to make do with a Stanier 2-6-0. The 10.45am parcels from Euston terminates in No 1 Down Through, before setting back noisily into the Down Sidings behind a Crewe '5X'. Locals to Llandudno, Liverpool and Manchester keep the North bays busy, while a WR 'Manor' sneaks into No 2 Bay with the 12.50pm from Aberystwyth. Platform 2 accommodates the 3.50pm Birmingham–Manchester, rapidly followed by the

2.22pm Euston–Liverpool at 5.30 – a good bet for a Camden '7P'. Eight minutes later, an Edge Hill Pacific follows with the main 2.30 from Euston to Merseyside, not forgetting the last Northwich motor at 5.57pm!

West of England and London departures initially dominate on the up side. A Longsight Class 5 heads the 3.15pm Manchester–Plymouth into Platform 5, away at 4.20, preceded by the 3.10pm Liverpool–Cardiff at 4.09 behind a 'Crab' promoted to passenger duty. In Platform 4 the 8.55am Perth–Euston exchanges its Carlisle Pacific for a Camden '7P'. Then the 1.55pm Holyhead–Euston rolls into Platform 3, exchanging Holyhead's No 45110 for a Willesden sister. The 4.20pm to Leek sits in No 6 Bay behind a Stoke Fowler 2-6-4 tank. No 4 Platform then hosts the 10.50am Workington–Euston, with a Preston '5XP' going through. The Up Through is occupied from 4.28 to 4.37 while the 2.50pm Llandudno–Birmingham exchanges Crewe and Aston Class 5s. The 3.20pm local from Manchester terminates in Platform 6 and is then off to the carriage shed, while the 2.30pm Holyhead–Birmingham is next in Platform 3 with another exchange of Crewe and Aston locomotives. Platform 5 accommodates the 1.30pm Barrow–Crewe, followed by the 4.10pm Liverpool–Euston, with an Edge Hill 7P away at 5.02. Locals to Wellington and Stoke depart behind a '51xx' tank and a Stanier 2-6-4 tank respectively, before the 3.05pm Holyhead–Euston comes into Platform 3 behind Crewe's unrebuilt No 46148 *The Manchester Regiment*. The 4.35pm Manchester–Birmingham is into No 4 at 5.17pm, drawing well down with the 4.17pm Liverpool–Crewe terminating behind. The next half-hour is taken with locals to Shrewsbury and arrivals from Manchester, Chester and Northwich, and the return Calveley milk is got across to the Up Hill Sidings.

Only 40 trains are booked in the next two hours, so matters are beginning to wind down just a little! In No 7 Bay the 6.00pm to Carlisle is ready to go – a typical West Coast semi-fast of six coaches and three vans with a Preston 'Patriot'. The 8.00am Newquay–Manchester is expected in Platform 2 from 6.00 to 6.04pm, but the reality will be quite different. Locals from Stafford and for Chester and Manchester depart, and the 10.20am Kingswear–Manchester should be into Platform 1 at 6.20, with the rear Manchester portion away at 6.35. No sign yet. Behind the draught screens, Crewe has a good '5XP,

No 45586 *Mysore*, for the 6.37pm Carlisle parcels, her distinctive six-beater echoing through the trainsheds and off the Nantwich Road bridge as she gets the road 'main line', wheeling out of the Down Sidings and along No 1 Through Road.

The Newquay finally appears at 6.45pm – not doing too badly! Weary holidaymakers disembark, having been incarcerated for 10¾ hours, and it's work on Monday! The Kingswear is right behind, running down Platform 1 with a Crewe Class 5. The train is quickly split; the Liverpool portion gets away, then a Longsight 2-6-4 tank sets back onto the Manchester coaches and the long-suffering passengers are on the last lap at 7.00pm. The station staff take a welcome 10-minute break before the 4.15pm Euston–Liverpool calls at Platform 2 'right time' at 7.11. The Edge Hill men are working home and it's a joy to hear their 'Royal Scot' pick up the 15 coaches and set off on the final 30 miles to Merseyside. A Crewe Class 5 follows with the 6.05pm Birmingham–Liverpool, its North Wales connection, the 7.50pm Llandudno, sitting in No 7 Bay with yet another Crewe Class 5.

On the up side a Crewe 'Black Five' emerges from the Up Hill Sidings with the 6.05pm Willesden parcels, getting away to the Up Relief just ahead of the 5.25pm Liverpool–Euston 'flyer', the 'Red Rose', a job for a good Camden Pacific, booked in Platform 4 from 6.10 to 6.15. The 5.11pm local from Manchester terminates in No 6. This and the 4.40pm Manchester Exchange–Crewe ECS on the Up Through provide two quick departures for the carriage shed. Platform 3 hosts the 4.00pm Bangor–Birmingham for 38 minutes, exchanging Chester and Crewe Class 5s. The 5.50pm Manchester–Euston comes smartly into Platform 4 at 6.33 behind a Camden '7P'. Can the signalman now sneak the 4.43pm Speke Junction–Longport Class F through the station without caning the up 'Midday Scot'? Today there is a sturdy ex-works '8F' on the job. With Stoke men working home on a Saturday evening they are not hanging around and clear the Up Through by 6.50. The 'Scot' runs down No 4 Platform 'right time' at 6.55pm behind Crewe's No 46235 *City of Birmingham*, and shed sister No 46248 *City of Leeds* is in the engine line at the south end waiting to take over.

Then the station resounds to the 'one *two* three four' 'Wessie beat' of 'Super D' No 49454 as she comes energetically across the layout with the 4.45pm Mold Junction–Crewe Class H, bound for the North

Stafford Sidings. Next into No 4 is the terminating 12.14pm from Perth, a job for a Crewe unrebuilt 'Scot'. The 5.05pm Blackpool–Euston follows with a Kingmoor '5XP', this being the last principal up service of the day. Over in No 3 Bay No 7819 *Hinton Manor* is sizzling on two coaches (and not many more passengers!) forming the 7.45pm to Whitchurch; amazingly this service will survive until early 1965. Over on Platform 5, the 7.10pm Manchester–Cardiff arrives at 7.58, an important mail and parcels service that does not leave until 8.33pm.

There are still 33 trains to go before we leave the scene at 10.00pm. Trains are still rolling in from the West Country on the down side. The 10.05am Penzance–Liverpool is due in Platform 2 at 8.05am, but she's 30 minutes late – not too much of a platforming problem, as it is now fairly quiet. The 5.05pm Euston–Blackpool occupies Platform 1 from 8.19 to 8.21 with a Camden '7P', leaving a portion for stations to Preston, which leaves at 8.27pm behind a Preston Class 5. The 5.20pm Euston–Holyhead follows immediately, from 8.28 until 8.35pm, exchanging Crewe and Chester locomotives, probably '5XPs'. The Penzance shows at last and is diverted into Platform 2. Hard on its heels is the 4.50pm Cardiff–Manchester, booked in No 1 from 8.42 to 8.49, and the 12.30pm Paignton-Manchester, which slips into No 2 Platform 15 minutes late at 8.57. The 6.00pm Euston–Manchester goes by on the Down Through at 8.55, followed by Edge Hill's returning No 46207 with the 16-coach down 'Merseyside Express', safety valves simmering, injector on, everything in apple-pie order, 2 minutes early at 9.03pm – a magnificent spectacle in the setting sunlight. Platform 2 now has two Euston–Heyshams from 9.18 to 9.39, the second being the 'Ulster Express'. A Carnforth '5XP' heads the first, with a Preston engine on the second. Locals depart in all directions in the next 20 minutes, but for once the down line is free of principal expresses.

Matters are quieter in the up direction, but Platform 6 is still needed for the 6.05pm Blackpool–Stoke and 6.15pm Llandudno–Derby as late holidaymakers stream home. The 8.33pm Cardiff is still in Platform 5 with the 8.20pm Bristol in No 4 when the 6.03pm Wyre Dock-Broad Street fish rolls along the Up Through at 8.21 to change its Preston 'Patriot' for a Willesden Class 5. Close behind is the 6.03pm Ellesmere Port–Etruria tanks, which makes a noisy passage of ringing big ends and

clashing buffers through Platform 6 behind Crewe South's No 48252. A '51xx' tank heads the 8.50pm to Wellington from No 2 Bay, as the 8.50pm Euston parcels eases out of the Up Hill Sidings and makes for the Up Through behind a Crewe '7P'. The next hour provides a chance to move some freight – an Edge Hill–Birmingham Class E, the 6.24pm Wyre Dock–Crewe fish, a Crewe–Birmingham parcels from the Up Hill Sidings, and the 8.50pm Edge Hill–Camden Class D completing the sequence. Plenty for 'Black Five' enthusiasts here!

As we stagger home with our bulging notebooks, it is worth reflecting that Crewe has dealt with some 229 down and 207 up passenger and parcels trains, and possibly another 40 or 50 reliefs and excursions. Additionally some ten passenger trains and numerous reliefs in both directions have been booked to use the Independent Lines, mostly North Wales services using the connection to the west of the station from the North Junction to Salop Goods Junction. Even on a summer Saturday some 75 down and 105 up freights are booked into and out of Basford Hall Yard, many being just partially observed as they whistle for the tunnels under the North Junction. Countless trains have changed engines, and the station pilots – 'Jinties' – have been constantly on the go, attaching, detaching, making up and breaking up parcels trains.

At the time of our visit Crewe is also a huge interchange for through van traffic. This is especially true in the down direction and during the soft fruit season. In June there can be up to four specials per night of French strawberries or Tamar Valley fruit arriving via Shrewsbury. Others come via Willesden carrying fruit from Kent and Hampshire. Crewe is also the natural outlet for parcels traffic from the Western Region via both Wellington and Shrewsbury. The vans arrive on various services between 7.00pm and 6.00am, and the station pilots are continually busy remarshalling them for forward despatch on the early parcels trains to northern destinations. More vans arrive between 3.00 and 6.00am; perishable and urgent traffic will make the early morning services, but there are often 30 or more vans left for later despatch.

On the up side the 12.01am parcels from Glasgow to Euston, due at 7.43am, often leaves about eight vehicles to be unloaded in Platform 6 with fish from Aberdeen. Pigeon traffic amounts to 30-40 vans per week, with complete special trains running on Thursday or Friday nights. Originating

in Cumberland, Lancashire or South Wales, the trains are remarshalled at Crewe and made up into further complete trains, often for the West Country. Palethorpe's sausage vans are also a familiar sight attached to expresses and parcels services, while the arrival of a banana boat at Garston Docks will result in numerous banana specials to London and elsewhere – a favourite occupation for 'Patriots'.

Behind the scenes an army of railwaymen has been keeping the job going. Operating Managers will have been watching anxiously as locomotive and coaching resources are stretched to the limit. The timetable is theoretically set for an optimum number of trains, but there are many extras on top of this and delays will be inevitable. Control will be keeping an eye on the overall picture, but the crucial decisions will be taken by the Regulators and their signalmen in the North and South boxes, whose job it is to make instant decisions about conflicting movements, and how best to keep the service moving. Platform Inspectors will be rushing around ensuring the expeditious despatch of trains, certain in the knowledge that there will be another one following immediately, and the reassuring ring of the Carriage & Wagon Examiner's hammer resounds from every long-distance train stopped in the station. Porters are busy with luggage and parcels, and the inevitable distracted passengers, while with so many engine changes shunters are like gold-dust! In the North and South sheds, fitters are struggling with running repairs against ever-tightening turn-rounds, while perspiring enginemen fight the incessant battle with preparation and disposal – cleaning the 50 square feet of firebox on a 'Princess' Pacific after a 243-mile run from Glasgow without a rocking grate is no picnic! Very few of the good people of Crewe wish to have the railway for a hobby as well as an occupation – given all the activity of the last 24 hours their attitude is not surprising, and many of them are surrounded by the sounds of the railway in their off-duty moments as well!

So that was Crewe. The station remains an important junction, but operational methods with modern trains are infinitely simpler, as the swathes of lifted track and empty platforms since the £14 million 1985 re-modelling of the station testify. The modern railway, now deprived of much traditional traffic, is undoubtedly a much more efficient, if not quite so captivating, organisation, and the platform 'congregations' are now much smaller.

4. CREWE TO WARRINGTON: THE LINE DESCRIBED

From Crewe, level quadruple tracks lead through open country past Coppenhall and Minshull Vernon, after which the line generally descends towards Weaver Junction. The Shropshire Union Canal is crossed as the line is carried boldly on embankments at the approach to Winsford, whence a brief double-track section in cutting leads to Winsford Junction, where the Over & Wharton branch converged from the left. Onwards to Verdin Sidings the layout was once six tracks past the former salt works sites on the down side. Double track recommences through the cutting leading to Vale Royal Viaduct over the deeply incised Weaver, and a long, deep cutting leads past Hartford to Hartford Junction, where the CLC Chester line crosses overhead with its north-to-east connecting spur on the up side. As the countryside opens out quadruple track follows to Acton Bridge, past the 1953 Gorstage Yard on the up side, once connected by the private Wallerscote Light Railway as the outlet for ICI's Wallerscote Works. There are fine views in both directions along the Weaver valley from the Dutton Viaduct leading to Weaver Junction, 16.2 miles from Crewe.

Here the Liverpool line diverges west via a flying junction, the first in the country. The opening of the direct Liverpool line in 1869 was a major improvement, ending the detour via Newton and giving direct access to Runcorn and the chemical industries of south-west Lancashire. The main line then rises at 1 in 330 before falling at 1 in 180 through wooded country alongside the Trent & Mersey Canal to Preston Brook. A descent at 1 in 112 takes the line under the Bridgewater Canal, and it then falls at 1 in 567 through open country past Norton Crossing, with the Birkenhead Joint Line from Chester to Warrington crossing overhead. The site of Moore water troughs is next, followed immediately by that of Moore station, before a rise at 1 in 135 to the Manchester Ship Canal bridge and the junction with the Chester line at Acton Grange. Panoramic views to the west open out before the final descent at 1 in 135 amidst industrial surroundings and railway yards to Warrington Bank Quay, 24.2 miles from Crewe.

5. CREWE TO WARRINGTON: TRAFFIC AND TRAINS

The initial Grand Junction Railway timetable of 1837 saw six daily passenger trains each way. Four were 1st Class only, serving principal stations including Hartford, and took 4½ hours from Liverpool to Birmingham. Two 'mixed' trains called at all stations and took an hour longer. From Hartford, horse buses served Knutsford, Tarporley and Chester, with Runcorn similarly served from Preston Brook.

From 1846 the line was absorbed into the London & North Western Railway, one of the most powerful industrial concerns in the country, whose formidable Chairman, Sir Richard Moon, nevertheless declared that 40mph was a respectable average for any express! So the line was worked by small 2-2-2 and 2-4-0 'Crewe Goods' types and was reluctantly drawn into the 1888 'Race to the North' when the Webb Compounds and 'Precedent' 2-4-0s saw the London–Edinburgh time standardised at 8½ hours. Within ten years, however, 0-6-0 and 0-8-0 locomotives were handling freight, and a thorough-going tradition of hard running was developing on the passenger side, immortalised by the incredible performance of the 2-4-0 *Hardwicke* in the 1895 'race', when the 141 miles to Carlisle were covered in an amazing 126 minutes, with the London–Aberdeen time down to 8½ hours.

Succeeding years saw a veritable pageant of locomotive spectacles. Picture the elegant Edwardian 'Tourist' expresses with their privileged clientele heading north for the 'Glorious Twelfth' behind an 'Experiment' or 'Prince of Wales' 4-6-0, or in 1913 the 'Claughton' *Ralph Brocklebank* taking the 360-ton 'Corridor' to Carlisle in just 142 minutes. During the First World War LNWR enginemen kept peacetime schedules with wartime loads, while LNWR 0-8-0s trudged endlessly in both directions with munitions and supplies. In 1910 the famous Caledonian Railway 4-6-0 *Cardean* ran trials to Crewe, and in 1926 came an outstanding trial performance by the GWR's *Launceston Castle*, presaging the introduction of the 'Royal Scot' 4-6-0s.

In 1928 the LMS cheekily pre-empted the LNER's non-stop 'Flying Scotsman' by running the 'Royal Scot' specially non-stop to Glasgow behind No 6113 *Cameronian*, and to Edinburgh behind Compound No 1054. The zenith of steam came in November 1936 when No 6201 *Princess Elizabeth* came thundering through Minshull Vernon at more than 90mph on her 5hr 44min Glasgow–Euston epic, not eclipsed until the 1974 electrification. Her sisters were daily working wonders on the heavy 'Midday Scot', while the streamlined 'Duchesses' streaked across country with the 6½-hour 'Coronation Scot'. The ultimate came on a wild winter's Sunday in February 1939 when No 6234 *Duchess of Abercorn* set out for Glasgow with her 604-ton test train to establish the highest horsepower (3,333ihp) ever recorded with a British steam locomotive. After the war years of slow schedules, gargantuan loads and full line occupation, which saw the railways virtually flogged to death, the 1948 Locomotive Exchanges saw visits by an LNER 'A4' and SR 'West Country' and 'Merchant Navy' Pacifics. Under British Railways, a slow recovery led to a steam renaissance in the late 1950s. The star turns were the Edge Hill 'Princesses' on the 14-17-coach 'Merseyside Express', with the ever-capable 'Duchesses' on the heavy Anglo-Scottish trains, as well as the high-speed 'Caledonian', on which No 46244 staged a 6¼-hour post-war record in June 1957.

An essential feature of the 1950s was the indispensable role of the converted '7P' 4-6-0s in substituting for Pacifics (of which there were only 39), and in powering the great majority of 'second line' principal expresses to Carlisle, Fylde and Furness. The '5XP' 4-6-0s were also employed on many important long-distance workings –

the Birmingham-Edinburgh trains for example – and many shorter-distance services such as Birmingham–Liverpool/ Manchester and trains to the West Country. Stanier's 'Black Fives' also took much of this work, and were almost universal on the extensive Saturday excursions to the Fylde. Liverpool locals witnessed a great variety of power – usually Class 5s, occasionally 2-6-4 tanks and often a whole range of locomotives recently outshopped from Crewe.

The arrival of the English Electric Type 4 diesels in 1959 signalled profound changes, and by 1962 all the principal services were booked (officially at least) for diesel power. Failures and relief services kept surviving '8P' and '7P' locomotives on semi-regular 'Top Link' work until the summer of 1964, when O. S. Nock was still able to record 'some of the best running ever' north of Crewe when *Duchess of Rutland* substituted for a diesel on the down 'Midday Scot'. By this time Brush Type 4 2,750hp diesel-electrics were arriving in large numbers, and in September came the shock withdrawal of the remaining 'Duchesses', while the '7P' 4-6-0s had largely disappeared by the following summer. 'Black Fives' and 'Britannias' took the final curtain-call north of Crewe in steam's neglected years to the autumn of 1967, until which time a surprisingly large number of trains remained steam-hauled, especially on summer weekends.

The Liverpool line had been electrified from 1 January 1962, but total revolution came with the Euston–Liverpool/ Manchester electrification in April 1966 when the Class 86s and their new rakes of Mark 2 stock really did herald a new era of rail travel. The 1970s also saw a new era in speed to the north, with double-headed Class 50 diesels, followed at last by the 1974 electrification to Glasgow. Alas, the innovative Advanced Passenger Train of the mid-1980s suffered from lack of political will for final development, but in 2004 the 'Voyagers' and 'Pendolinos' arrived and a new era of 125mph running began.

It should not be forgotten that, until the last 30 years, freight, parcels and mail traffic was the major feature of this railway. Several substantial parcels trains ran daily between Crewe and Glasgow, together with the up and down 'West Coast Postal Specials'. Through merchandise freight was absolutely incessant until heavily rationalised or lost to the roads from the 1970s. In steam days such trains, running in

braked or loose-coupled format, dominated the scene, with the fierce staccato of 'Black Fives' or 'Crabs' and latterly 9Fs pounding away at 50-60mph with their 40-wagon loads, echoing across the countryside round the clock, with the service still mainly steam-powered until Crewe South shed closed in November 1967. Stanier 2-6-0s and 2-8-0s also took a major role with these trains, as well as working mineral services, of which there were comparatively few. The last LNWR survivors – the 'Super D' 0-8-0s – were also prominent on such work as late as 1961. Before resignalling in 1961, line occupation was intense, with long queues of up to five freights waiting to leave the Down Loop at Winsford. Today's increasing numbers of air-braked Freightliners and company trains provide stark contrast to such activity, but also certain evidence of the railway's potential given the inevitable future gridlock on the roads.

In 1900 rail traffic was so heavy that the LNWR made plans for quadruple track all the way to Preston. The 1906 Crewe remodelling was part of this process, and the north main line was widened to Moretons Crossing, Coppenhall, in 1908. A similar widening had been undertaken between Winsford Junction and Verdin Sidings in 1898, but financial problems in the Edwardian years and the First World War saw further widenings between Moretons Crossing and Winsford and Hartford Junction and Acton Bridge undertaken by the LMS in 1927. Curiously, the comparatively easy section between Winsford and Winsford Junction was never widened, but the Vale Royal and Dutton viaducts, together with the deep cutting at Hartford, discouraged further widening to Weaver Junction.

Of the local stations, Monks Coppenhall was rapidly superseded by Crewe and closed in May 1840. Minshull Vernon, Preston Brook and Moore became little more than wayside halts enjoying a sparse service and chequered histories. Minshull Vernon closed on 2 March 1942; Preston Brook, having lost its horse bus service to Runcorn in 1869, followed on 1 March 1948; and Moore closed finally on 21 April 1949. Winsford and Hartford retained their original GJR buildings until rebuilt for the 1962 electrification, but Acton Bridge was rebuilt in 1925 as part of preparations for quadrupling. Hartford had more commodious accommodation because of its original function as a road interchange. Its proximity to Northwich and the ICI works meant that for many years several

intermediate expresses were booked to call, and the platforms were lengthened in 1961 to facilitate these stops.

After 1869 the main local service was to Liverpool, that to the north being quite sparse – only two or so trains daily by the 1960s – together with the very limited Acton Bridge–Warrington service, which offered some very doubtful connections, disappearing finally in June 1965. Liverpool locals included some trains that came from Shrewsbury or Stoke, or which worked through to Rugby; some started from Ditton Junction. Ex-works locomotives frequently appeared on these diagrams, some of which covered West of England trains to Shrewsbury, a wide range of power from Pacifics to 2-6-4 tanks being involved. The service would almost certainly have disappeared beyond Runcorn in the Beeching rationalisation, but the 1962 Liverpool electrification and the designation of Winsford as a Liverpool overspill settlement saw the service retained with an hourly frequency. Locals to the north survived until the May 1966 timetable, when many changes were made to traditional service patterns. For many years Crewe–Liverpool locals were worked by Class 304 EMUs. The line currently forms part of Central Trains' Birmingham-Liverpool service, with an alternate-hour Crewe–Liverpool 'shuttle' by Arriva on which Class 158s and 170s predominate.

The LNWR weekday winter timetable for 1921/2 found 88 passenger trains, 60 of them expresses, booked through Winsford, an average of one every 16½ minutes throughout the day. Down trains included eight Anglo-Scottish services, four overnight to Glasgow, Edinburgh, Inverness and Perth, the long-standing 9.15am Crewe–Perth, and the 10.00am and 1.30pm ('The Corridor') from Euston to Glasgow. Seven trains ran to Fylde or Furness destinations, including the 4.45pm 'Belfast Boat Express' to Fleetwood and Barrow. Liverpool had six services to London, two of them overnight, and there were six trains from Plymouth or Bristol to Liverpool and three from Birmingham. Locals included the 6.15am from Crewe to Carlisle, the 11.55am to Warrington, and the 8.45pm to Wigan, with motor trains from Over & Wharton to Newton le Willows, Hartford and Acton Bridge, together with six conveniently spaced Liverpool locals. Up services were very similar, but with only three West of England trains from Liverpool. Locals included trains from St Helens and Earlestown to Over & Wharton, and seven from Liverpool, including the 12.28pm from Ditton Junction.

The LMS Summer service of 1939 was much busier, with 135 passenger services, 102 expresses, an average of one train every 6½ minutes on weekdays, with another 20 or 30 'extras' on Saturdays. On the down line there were 18 Anglo-Scottish trains, headed by the 6½-hour 'Coronation Scot', and the fast but heavy 'Royal Scot' and 'Midday Scot'. Also featured was the 9.27am Crewe–Perth, a lavish overnight service including the 'Royal Highlander', the 7.20am Euston–Inverness, together with the Euston–Stranraer 'Northern Irishman' and day and night services from Birmingham. Fifteen expresses ran to Fylde and Furness, the Fleetwood boat train having been replaced by the 'Ulster Express' to Heysham, and Blackpool, Preston, Workington and

Windermere enjoying a much improved service. Seven expresses ran to Merseyside, with four conditional paths for ocean liner expresses to Liverpool Riverside. Four West-to-North and six expresses between Crewe and Liverpool completed the picture. Down locals to Carlisle included the 5.35am and 6.17am from Crewe, and the 5.51pm to Windermere. Motor trains ran from Wharton to Runcorn, Warrington and Acton Bridge, and a return working from Warrington to Crewe. The unadvertised 5.57am Crewe–Hartford workmen's service continued as the 8.20am to Warrington, and there were nine locals to Liverpool including the 6.40am from Shrewsbury. Only four down parcels trains ran, the most important being the 2.40am Euston–Carlisle 'Horse and Cart'.

There were 72 expresses similarly

arranged on the up service. Up locals included the 6.25am from Carlisle, fast from Warrington (it was all-stations under BR). There were seven Liverpool–Crewe workings, two from Ditton Junction. Eight expresses linked Liverpool and London, including the 5.25pm 'Liverpool Flyer' (the 'Red Rose' of BR days) and the 10.10am 'Merseyside Express', together with two conditional paths for boat trains. Seven parcels trains ran, including the time-served 8.35am Carlisle–Crewe 'Horse and Cart'. The 1.55pm Aberdeen-Broad Street and 9.37am Carlisle–Birmingham fish trains and the 3.20pm Carlisle–Euston milk completed the picture, not forgetting the up and down 'Postal Specials', 8.30pm from Euston and 6.35pm from Glasgow, which were booked to pass each other between Winsford and Winsford Junction.

6. NORTH FROM CREWE

Left:
Crewe Coal Yard, 20 August 1938
Streamlined 'Coronation' class Pacific No 6223 *Princess Alice* bursts under Hungerford Road bridge at the head of the 10.30am Euston–Liverpool express. The yard, otherwise known as Cumberland Wharf, was opened by the North Staffordshire Railway in the 1870s. The NSR had set up its own loco shed and marshalling yard alongside the Stoke line after 1865, and reached the Coal Yard, a useful outlet for domestic coal from the North Staffordshire Coalfield, by running powers through Crewe station. The yard remained open until the 1970s. The photograph appears to have been taken from the pre-1940 signalbox.
F. A. Lewis collection

Left:
Crewe Coal Yard, 10 April 1959
There were actually three yards here – the Crewe Co-operative Society Cumberland Coal Wharf (far right beyond the signalbox), the NSR's Thomas St Wharf (on the right), and the LNWR's Cobden St Wharf and sidings (left). Ascending on the left is the Down Liverpool Independent Line, routed under the North Junction from March 1902. The junction with the fast lines was controlled from a box built astride the down lines near the signal gantry, which opened in 1902. The new box (middle right), built to ARP standards, opened on 10 December 1939 and is still in use. On the left is Crewe market, where shopping was thrillingly interrupted by passing trains, tantalisingly just out of sight. Note the masts going up for the forthcoming Liverpool electrification.
H. Townley, C. M. & J. M. Bentley collection

Right:
A plan of the various sidings at Crewe Coal Yard in 1929.

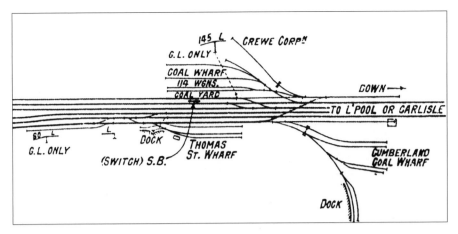

Right:
Crewe Coal Yard, 18 March 1905
LNWR locomotives were not renowned for the efficiency of their brakes, and Webb 17-inch coal engine No 1333 appears to have spectacularly 'run out of road' in a shunting movement at the Coal Yard. Note the chains around the boiler securing the engine from an even more spectacular fate, and the cleanliness of a humble goods locomotive in those days of ample cleaners and minimum staff wages.
B. Matthews collection

Below:
Crewe Coal Yard, c1910
At the northern extremity of the yard, a Whale 19-inch Goods 4-6-0 makes a vigorous recovery, having been turned out on the Down Fast line with an express goods, while a Class G 0-8-0 stands at signals on the Up Slow line, possibly while shunting at Cumberland Wharf. The headshunt for Cobden Street sidings is on the right. *LNWR Society 2175*

Left:
Monks Coppenhall, June 1934
Soon to be superseded by the influx of new Stanier locomotives, an LNWR combination of 'George V' 4-4-0 and 'Prince of Wales' 4-6-0 passes the site of Monks Coppenhall station, closed in May 1840, with a down express. The engines may be substituting for a 'Royal Scot' on the down 'Midday Scot', with its GWR Plymouth–Glasgow through coach, or alternatively the train may be the 8.45am Plymouth–Liverpool West to North service. *E. R. Morten, courtesy of J. R. Morten*

Right:
Coppenhall Junction, 21 August 1957
'Duchess' Pacific No 46247 *City of Liverpool* coasts across Coppenhall Moss with the 13-coach up 'Red Rose', the crack evening service from Liverpool to Euston, always a source of good running by Edge Hill's Top Link. Coppenhall Junction box and signals are in the background. The line was quadrupled to Moretons Crossing in 1908, as part of the 1906 Crewe remodelling. The flat landscape hereabouts, now developed for housing to the west, was a welcome sight to Crewe men returning from tiring, often overnight lodging turns to Glasgow and Perth. *D. M. C. Hepburne-Scott, Rail Archive Stephenson*

Left:
Coppenhall Junction, 30 September 1959
An unrebuilt 'Patriot' 4-6-0 heads an up fitted freight past the late-LNWR-pattern signalbox, which opened on 12 June 1927, superseding the 25-lever Coppenhall Junction box of 1908, which in turn had replaced the original Moretons Crossing box. The 1927 box was 878 yards south of Moretons Crossing (which was replaced with a footbridge in 1908), and closed with the introduction of multiple-aspect signalling on 5 June 1961. The 1961 box was 650 yards north, almost at the original Moretons location, and also signalled the Minshull Vernon area. The junction between Up and Down Fast and Slow lines was abolished on 10 September 1979. *T. Booth collection*

Right:
A plan of the pre-quadrupling Minshull Vernon station, 4.9 miles from Crewe, dated December 1909. The GJR optimistically opened this station where the Nantwich–Middlewich turnpike crossed the line in a totally rural situation. Few passengers were seen and the extensive land taken for a goods yard was never used.

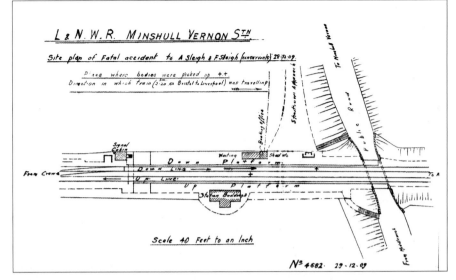

Right:

Minshull Vernon, 16 August 1958
Until 1961 the deserted platforms of the closed station offered grandstand views of passing traffic. The LMR never really had enough Pacifics, and in the 1950s many expresses loaded very heavily and were willingly strengthened to meet the traffic on offer. Much of the load fell to the ever-willing 'Converted Scots' and the overworked '5XPs'. Double-heading with '2P' 4-4-0s was often resorted to, and they could be a mixed blessing! Here '2P' No 40657 and 'Royal Scot' No 46156 *The South Wales Borderers* tackle 16 coaches on what is probably W106, the Saturday 10.06am Glasgow–Euston relief (usually a Pacific job).
E. R. Morten, courtesy of J. R. Morten

Right:

Minshull Vernon, 16 August 1958
An alternative with heavy expresses was to use two 'Black Fives'. Two of the class, Caprotti No 44750 leading, front 17 coaches on what is possibly the specially strengthened 10.10am Edinburgh–Birmingham on this peak Saturday. Quadrupling to Weaver Junction was authorised in 1900, but never fully completed. Coppenhall Junction to Winsford was widened by the LMS from 12 June 1927, and the second Minshull Vernon station can be glimpsed behind the engines. After closure, the buildings were in engineers' use for many years, being demolished in the 1970s. A sign on the door read 'Please sound horn, Driver, Fireman and Guard in Verdin Arms' (a nearby hostelry!). The late-LNWR-pattern signalbox of 1927 closed with the introduction of colour light signalling in June 1961. 1958 was the first year that your 10-year-old author was allowed out 'solo' trainspotting, and many captivating hours were spent sitting on the oil drums on the right.
E. R. Morten, courtesy of J. R. Morten

Above:

Minshull Vernon, *c*1958

The safety-valves roar and no doubt there is some pithy Scouse humour flying around the cab of No 46207 *Princess Arthur of Connaught* as she is checked by signals. The driver stares intently for the Starter to come off, and the customary gargantuan load of the up 'Merseyside Express' follows. With never fewer than 15 coaches, this train was the highlight of your author's first trainspotting summer in 1958, and for sheer spine-tingling entertainment it could not be beaten! *A. Wilkinson*

Left:

Minshull Vernon, 2 July 1964

The 1962 electrification removed almost all traces of the station, to the great disappointment of local enthusiasts! AC electric No E3081 heads the down 'Shamrock', the 16.30 Euston–Liverpool, past the now vanished platforms. Electric locomotives were working between Liverpool and Stafford at this time. *A. Wilkinson*

Above:

Minshull Vernon, *c*1958

The 1927 quadrupling was accompanied by LNWR signalling, and the examples on the left still made a brave show in 1958. On the left is the Down Slow to Fast Starter, with a Calling-on arm for the Down Goods line to Winsford, worked under Permissive Block regulations. 'Jubilee' No 45633 *Aden* approaches with the 10.53am Workington–Euston service. *H. Townley, C. M. & J. M. Bentley collection*

Below:

Clive Back Lane, Winsford, 24 February 1966

In the autumn of 1964 the 10.35 Euston–Carlisle service reverted to regular steam haulage north of Crewe, neatly complementing a very pleasant early afternoon 'steam session' as it was preceded by the 1.16pm Carlisle parcels and the 1.20pm Crewe–Carlisle Class 4, and followed by the 11.20 Oxley–Carlisle express freight, with the 11.20 Windermere–Crewe passenger and several freights on the up line. On a fair February afternoon, 'Britannia' No 70022 *Tornado* makes a fine spectacle as she nears Winsford. *A. Wilkinson*

Above:
South of Winsford, 26 February 1952
The Winsford Down Home signals disappear into the smoke haze as Camden's 'Duchess' No 46242 *City of Glasgow*, resplendent in the short-lived BR passenger blue livery, pounds southwards at 1 in 300 with the up 'Royal Scot', at that time a mixture of BR and Stanier vehicles in carmine and cream livery. The local ganger is 'walking his length' in the distance – no high-visibility clothing then! The Down Goods line saw several incidents of over-running in Permissive Block days, and the exit was moved southwards on electrification. This has not stopped incidents entirely, however, as the 1999 collision between a down express and an errant 'Pacer' evidenced. *E. R. Morten, courtesy of J. R. Morten*

Left:
Approaching Winsford, 26 June 1964
This was the author's 'siesta spot' south of Winsford (note the convenient tree providing summer shade). Not a 'Super D', but 'WD' 2-8-0 No 90686 – rather a rare bird in these parts – approaches the Home signals on the Down Slow line with the 1.20pm Crewe–Bamfurlong freight, upgraded to Class 5 category. *A. Wilkinson*

7. WINSFORD

Right:

Winsford, 12 June 1962

Not perfectly sharp, but an important occasion captured with a Box Brownie: 'Princess' Pacific No 46200 *The Princess Royal* speeds southwards, picking up lost time with the return RCTS 'Aberdeen Flyer' special. She was 3 hours late and the photographer had given up, but she whistled for the station, allowing just enough time to scramble back up the embankment. Only three years earlier this would have been a daily event with the 'Merseyside Express', but now these first Stanier Pacifics had only three months of service left – very much a time of change.
A. Wilkinson

Below:

Winsford, 23 March 1967

Both the photographer and Class 5 No 44736 do battle with a fresh south-westerly as the loco heads an express freight (probably 4V86, the 03.29 Carlisle–Stoke Gifford) onto the Up Slow line. Winsford Station box in the background, new in 1927, closed on 28 October 1972, its functions being absorbed by Winsford Junction; a ground-frame-controlled crossover remained until 9 November 1986. This is the site of the 1999 collision referred to on the previous page. The rebuilt station and new road bridge of 1960 are in the background. *A. Wilkinson*

Above:
Winsford, 16 April 1955
Stanier 'Duchess' No 46237 *City of Bristol* speeds across Rilshaw Lane underbridge with a 14-coach up express. The station is in the middle distance with the trap siding for the Down Goods line, terminating just short of the underbridge. On at least two occasions over-running down freights almost deposited themselves into the lane, hence the present Slow Line exit, much further south. The author's perch on the Rilshaw Lane railway fence is just beyond the engine's left buffer. *G. W. Sharpe, A. Wilkinson collection*

Below:
Winsford, 10 October 1959
The station was originally in open countryside, a mile from the town centre. This view from a Liverpool local shows Rilshaw Lane railway cottages, the up Starting signals for entry to the four-track section onwards to Crewe, then the station overbridge with Nun House bridge beyond. On the right is the Railway Hotel, subsequently and incongruously renamed the Brighton Belle, complete with Pullman car, and the original station approach from the east, abandoned in 1961. *H. C. Casserley*

Right:

Winsford, July 1960

Wellingborough's Class 9F 2-10-0 No 92058, fresh from overhaul at Crewe, drifts out of the Down Goods line with a through freight, possibly the 2.20pm Crewe–Bamfurlong. The Winsford Down Home signals are in the distance, and electrification preparations have begun on the right. *A. Wilkinson*

Right:

Winsford, c1958

'Duchess' Pacific No 46237 *City of Bristol* bursts under the A54 roadbridge with the up 'Caledonian', the high-speed 6¾-hour service between Glasgow and London introduced in 1957. The modest GJR 'small station' buildings of 1837, replicated at Minshull Vernon, are supplemented by a standard LNWR waiting shelter on the down side. Behind the exhaust was a large poster hoarding, the supports of which provided an ideal vantage point for locospotters, not always appreciated by the station master! *H. Hodgkinson, A. Wilkinson collection*

Below:

An LMS plan of Winsford station dated 21 September 1938.

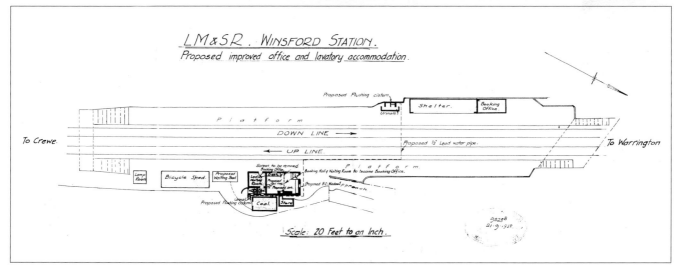

Left:
Winsford, July 1960
Standard LNWR huts and a cycle shed enhance the original GJR up-side buildings, while an old coach body on the down platform accommodated the local platelayers. 'Jubilee' No 45588 *Kashmir* arrives with the 6.10pm Crewe–Windermere, a popular service with the many Winsfordians employed at Crewe Works at that time. *A. Wilkinson*

Below:
Winsford, 20 May 1961
Watched by your author's locospotting schoolfriends, 'Patriot' No 45501 *St Dunstans* calls with the time-honoured 6.15am Carlisle–Crewe 'all stations'. The station has been newly rebuilt for the Crewe–Liverpool electrification inaugurated in June 1962. No 45501 was in her last months of service, although the 6.15am survived a few more years until the new electric timetable of April 1966, when many changes were made to traditional services. *A. Wilkinson*

Above:
Winsford coal yard and horse landing, *c*1955/6
Class 5 No 44704, with the 8.35am Carlisle–Crewe parcels (the 'Horse and Cart'), nears the station. On the left is the coal yard, closed in 1958, one of a series set up in early GJR days by R. Evans & Co, colliery owners of Haydock, who initially worked their own trains to Winsford. There was a fatal accident here on 17 July 1869 between a down excursion and a shunting coal train. Behind the engine is the site of the original Winsford signalbox of 1876-1927. The fields in the background will in a few years become the Winsford Industrial Estate. *T. Lewis, T. Booth collection*

Below:
Nun House bridge, 22 June 1933
'Royal Scot' No 6123 *Royal Irish Fusilier* heads the 8.35am Carlisle–Euston service halfway between Winsford and Winsford Junction. In the background are Winsford's up splitting Distants and Winsford Goods Yard down Distant, both typically tall LNWR specimens. Nearby was the site of British Railways' first serious accident, on 17 April 1948, when the 5.40pm Glasgow–Euston, headed by No 6207 *Princess Arthur of Connaught*, halted by the illicit use of the communication cord, was run into by No 6251 *City of Nottingham* on the up 'West Coast Postal' due to a signalling error. Sadly, 24 deaths resulted. *LCGB, Ken Nunn Collection*

8. WINSFORD SALT SIDINGS AND THE OVER & WHARTON BRANCH

Winsford was long-established as a salt-producing centre by the end of the 18th century, and demand peaked around 1880 when almost 800,000 tons were carried away on the River Weaver. Salt was traditionally produced by boiling brine (found in large quantities in the sedimentary strata underlying mid-Cheshire) in huge open metal pans heated by coal fires. Typically 2½ tons of coal were needed to yield 1 ton of high-quality salt, and, with the need to break the transport monopoly of the Weaver, there was lucrative traffic potential here for railways.

The Grand Junction Railway skirted Winsford across the edge of Wharton Common, traversing the salt beds and encouraging the development of salt works on the east bank of the river. Between 1845 and 1870 five works opened and were rail-connected between Kays Crossing (renamed Winsford Junction in 1898) and Verdin Sidings, access being provided from 1883 by a long siding on the down side of the main line, which was itself quadrupled to Verdin Sidings in 1898 as part of the LNWR plan for quadruple track between Crewe and Preston.

By 1870, two branches led from Kays Crossing to Stubbs National and three other works, and to William Lycett's Wharton Railway and River Works respectively. Previously, Lycett's Works (and possibly the Cheshire Amalgamated Works) were served, most probably from the early 1860s by a direct north-west-facing connection from the main line opposite Winsford Goods Yard. This would have been an inconvenience on a busy main line, and the Board of Trade also had strong reservations about facing connections. Thus by 1870 the Lycett branch had been diverted to form a northward-facing connection at Kays Crossing, and the remains of the original Lycett branch, disconnected from the main line, became Lycett's Coal Wharf, which, with its bridge under Wharton Road, remained open until about 1905. There was never a triangle at Winsford Junction, as is sometimes shown on old maps, since the 1870 connection to Kays Crossing superseded the original Lycett railway to the main line at Winsford Goods Yard.

Around 1880 the goods yard at Kays Crossing was established, and the first quarter-mile of the second (1870) Lycett branch became part of the mile-long LNWR salt branch to Liverpool and Birkenhead Works. This involved crossing the line of the original Lycett railway just before the second (Shaws Lane) bridge out from Kays Crossing. North of this point the Lycett line may have divided into two branches, one to the Railway and River Works, the other shown without track on the 1872 map, leading to the more northerly 'Wharton' (and Cheshire Amalgamated) Works. This latter roadbed may never have carried track, or it could be the lifted original Lycett line superseded in 1870 when the Lycett connection was diverted to Kays Crossing and the Amalgamated Works connection was diverted to join the National Works branch.

In 1882 the LNWR converted the Liverpool Works branch into its double track passenger line to Over & Wharton (for further details see the author's *Railways Across Mid Cheshire*, Vol 1, Foxline Publishing, 2001). Immediately beyond the second overbridge, the Brine branch diverged, running parallel for almost half a mile before descending through the river terrace to serve Uploont, Dudley and Birkenhead works, all rail-connected by 1882. In 1870 the Cheshire Lines Committee (CLC) branch from Cuddington had arrived on the west bank of the Weaver, and the constricted river valley was thenceforward packed with salt works on both banks. In 1888 most of the salt works owners joined the Salt Union (SU), an industrial grouping whose interests were inherited by ICI Ltd in 1940. However, the development of the vacuum process at Winsford in 1906 heralded a 60-year decline of traditional salt-making, and the last open pan works in Winsford closed in 1956.

Back in 1880 there was hardly any ground in the Weaver valley or on Wharton Common that was not heavily industrialised by smoke-belching saltworks. Together with the works came brine shafts, cisterns and associated pipework, coal dumps, mounds of clinker, wagon hoists and a really heterogeneous collection of practically constructed but hardly attractive buildings, creating an almost lunar landscape. The Weaver was alive with boats, and industrial locomotives fussed among the buildings on both sides of the river, and alongside express trains on the main line. The show was essentially over by the 1930s, and by the 1950s an air of desolation and mystery had replaced bustling activity, with just the occasional industrial shunter glimpsed amongst the decaying buildings surrounding the rusting tracks and branches lying largely undisturbed on Wharton Common.

With the exception of Newbridge, the works alongside the main line were the first to succumb. The small Bush's Works had closed by 1890, and Moulton Hall, Meadow and Bostock Works had all been demolished by 1930, but their sidings remained in situ until 1950-54, being required to relieve Winsford Junction yard during the war and latterly for wagon storage following works closures. The Salt Union wagon works was set up in 1883 in buildings to the south of Bostock Works and remained in operation until about 1950. Newbridge Works finally closed in 1954/5, and in 1956 Colin Stewart and Aerastone Ltd were still using part of the sidings, which finally disappeared in 1960-62. The independent down siding, which served all these works, was lifted in 1964/5.

On the National Works branch from Kays Crossing, Littlemeadow Works was an early casualty, being dismantled by 1913. By 1870 a sub-branch off this line led to the Cheshire Amalgamated Works, which, together with the National Works, remained at least partially open until 1954/5. The siding connections to these works were finally lifted in 1956, although the connection was not severed until the spring of 1965.

On the Wharton branch, the junction of the Lycett railway to the Railway and River Works and that to the Brine branch was controlled by Brine Branch box until 1925, when Brine Branch and Lycett Ground Frames were substituted. The group of works between Railway and River and the Amalgamated Works were then collectively known as 'Lycett Works', and from 1926 the SU designated the whole complex northwards to Newbridge as its 'North Works'. The Lycett complex seems to have struggled on until about 1955, traffic being handled latterly by a diesel tractor, with the sidings finally listed in 1956. On the Brine branch, the buildings of

Dudley Works were utilised by Colin Stewart Ltd, ground pottery dealers, whose siding still appeared in the 1966/7 Working Timetable. Uploont and Birkenhead Works, redesignated as 'South Works' in 1926, occupied major sites at river level, both having complex rail systems that were in use until about 1955.

Liverpool Works was alongside Over & Wharton station, being connected in the autumn of 1880. Immediately south and below was Island Works, closed by 1913, but its sidings, presumably used by Liverpool Works, were still listed in 1938. Liverpool Works closed in 1930, but its sidings were used to unload coal for Birkenhead Works, immediately below, which since 1888 had been the bunkering point for the SU steam barges. Also there was the SU engine shed, from which locomotives used BR tracks to access the

Brine branch salt works. The Running Agreement was terminated early in 1956, and from 1954 the South Works engine shed was located at Uploont Works.

The passenger service on the Wharton branch, dating from 1882, was always sparse – rarely more than six workings per day to Acton Bridge or South Lancashire towns – and usually worked by a Warrington 2-4-2 tank and motor set sub-shedded at Wharton. Services were suspended as a wartime economy between 1917 and 1920, and completely from 16 June 1947. The line was, however, served by two pick-up freights from Crewe and Warrington. The Crewe service, once the provider of North Staffordshire coal and distributor of salt via Basford Hall, ceased about 1961, while the thrice weekly Warrington train, concerned mainly with domestic coal and general traffic, ceased

on 10 June 1968. In the meantime the line had become relatively busy with rock salt traffic, especially after the CLC branch to the Rock Salt Mine closed in March 1967. The goods shed was demolished and the yard re-organised to facilitate the loading of rock salt from a substantial stockpile. Two trips ran daily from Northwich and trains were made up at Winsford Junction for despatch via the main line. By the 1980s block train working was the order of the day, and the line had to be closed in the winter of 1982/3 for relaying. Unfortunately, climatic change saw a series of much milder winters and the last salt trains ran in the winter of 1989/90. The branch was lifted in the spring of 1991, and the whole area in the vicinity of Winsford Junction redeveloped with housing, virtually obliterating most of the last traces of the salt industry and its railways.

Right:

Winsford goods yard, 3 April 1965
'Britannia' No 70019 *Lightning* lives up to her name, storming past the site of the goods yard and down-side Winsford Exchange signal box with the 10.35 Euston–Carlisle train. Sadly, it was on No 70052 working this train in June 1965 that Crewe Driver Wallace Oakes GC gave his life in bringing the train to a stand following a blow-back in the cab near Winsford.

The earthworks in the field on the right mark the remains of the original direct branch (*c*1860-70) to Lycett's Wharton Railway and River salt works, and also of Lycett's Coal Wharf of *c*1870-1905, accessed from the Over & Wharton branch. Winsford's original goods yard of 1837-*c*1925 was on the left, followed by sidings for the CWS bacon factory of 1937-61.
A. Wilkinson

Right:

Winsford goods yard, 3 October 1964
Class 5 No 45042 heads a Carlisle–Crewe express freight past the site of the goods yard and bacon factory sidings on the right. To the left of the engine's smokebox can be seen the parapet of one of the three distinctive blue-brick bridges on the Over & Wharton branch, which, with the Wharton road bridges on the Lycett branch and main line, gave the area its local title of 'Wharton Bridges'. The main-line bridge in the background was renewed in 1960 for electrification. *A. Wilkinson*

OLD PERMANENT WAY ON STONE BLOCKS, WINSFORD.

Left:
Winsford goods yard, 21 December 1904
This official LNWR postcard shows the original GJR permanent way of 62lb/yd rails on stone blocks still *in situ* in the yard. This was the town's original goods yard, being used until the 1920s, when facilities were concentrated at Over & Wharton. From 8 August 1937 the site was used for sidings serving the CWS bacon factory, and an LMS box on the down side replaced the up-side ground frame. The former was only spasmodically switched in and disappeared with the introduction of colour light signalling on 4 June 1961. *T. Booth collection*

Right:
Winsford Junction signalbox, c1930
Signalmen Tom Sanbach (right) and Ned Hulse (left) are working this 1898 box. It replaced the previous Kays Crossing box, located to the south of the wooden crossing in the foreground, which remained open until about 1960. Reprieved by economies at the time of the 1960s electrification, the box absorbed the functions of Verdin Sidings and Winsford Station boxes in 1972. Even more remarkably, in the late 1990s it took on the work of Weaver Junction, Acton Bridge and Hartford Junction! It has recently been refurbished and it will be some time yet before it is superseded by new signalling. *A. Sanbach collection*

Left:
Winsford Junction signalbox, 1905
Signalman Edward Edwards is at the levers, assisted by Signalman Sanbach. The track diagram shows the railway to be six tracks across northwards to Verdin Sidings – two down goods sidings and the quadruple main line. With the addition of the Wharton branch, a yard to be shunted, industrial locomotive movements and Kays Crossing, where Deakins Lane crossed the main line, this was a busy place! The fine array of LNWR block instruments and the Webb-Thompson frame with its 'stirrup grip' levers should be noted, as well as the lack of furniture – it was a much more comfortable place when your author knew it in the 1960s!
G. J. C. Griffiths, Winsford Historical Society

Right:

Winsford Junction, 21 February 1967
'Britain's New Railway.' After many vicissitudes, the Euston–Liverpool/Manchester electrification was inaugurated from 18 April 1966 and the 'sparks effect' was indeed phenomenal. Class AL6 electric No E3169 with new Mark II coaches tears effortlessly northwards with the 08.30 Euston–Liverpool service. In the foreground, the branch to the National and Cheshire Amalgamated Saltworks (c1870-1956) has just been lifted. The Wharton branch diverges in the centre, with the 161-wagon capacity yard on the right, which fell out of use by the mid-1970s when the rock salt traffic was turned over to block train working. *A. Wilkinson*

Left:

Cheshire Amalgamated Saltworks, *c*1905
Once a regular performer on the Amalgamated Works branch from Winsford Junction, and representative of the remarkable variety of industrial locomotives employed in the Winsford salt works, is this quaint Lewin 0-4-0ST *Wharton* of 1875, captured with a group of salt workers probably by local photographer E. Whitehead. *Wharton* departed for the Salt Union's South Durham works at Middlesbrough in 1907, and worked there until withdrawn in 1948. She was replaced by Robey 0-4-0ST *Liverton*, ex-Liverton Mines and SU Haverton Hill, which worked at Winsford until about 1925. *Courtesy of Mrs E. Morris*

Right:

Winsford Junction, 3 January 1967
Northwich '8F' No 48693 propels a raft of rock salt empties away from Winsford Junction for Over & Wharton. A train is already made up in the yard for despatch via the main line. Two trips per day were made to Northwich for distribution to more central and easterly destinations. *A. Wilkinson*

Left:
Winsford Junction, 23 April 1966
BR Class 2 2-6-0 No 78036 propels the RCTS's 'St George Railtour' from Nuneaton onto the Wharton branch. The embankment to the left of the locomotive is the line of the original direct branch from the main line to Lycett's Wharton Railway and River Works of *c*1860-70 (see page 35) and, by reversal, to Lycett's Coal Yard of *c*1870-1905. Just beyond the train is Shaws Lane bridge, the second of two bridges that replaced level crossings over the branch in 1882 when the passenger service began. The buildings and houses above the third carriage are at Over & Wharton station. *A. Wilkinson*

Right:
Shaws Lane bridge, Wharton branch, *c*1980
Looking towards Winsford Junction, Deakins Lane bridge is in the middle distance, with the CWS bacon factory beyond Wharton Road and to the east of the main line, top right. The trackbed to the left, and the line of fencing to the right, mark the line of the original Lycett branch from the main line at Winsford goods yard to the Railway and River Works, *c*1860-70. Middle left is the site of Brine Branch signal box, closed in 1925 and replaced by Lycett ground frame. The running line is on the left, and a long siding on the right. The Brine branch junction and ground frame were immediately behind Shaws Lane bridge. The branch to Railway and River (Lycett) Works closed *c*1956, and all this is now a housing estate. *G. J. C. Griffiths*

Left:
Wharton Common, 15 March 1959
The double-track branch was altered to single-line working from 1920 and the former up line became a long siding used in 1959/60 to store large numbers of 'Tilbury' 4-4-2 and 0-6-2 tanks and 'Super D' 0-8-0s awaiting scrapping. Traditionally stout railway wooden fencing (remember it?) surrounds the desolate line of locos, mostly from South Wales. Nat Lane bridge is in the background, and the Brine branch descends towards the Weaver on the right. Over & Wharton station is just around the corner to the left. This was a captivating scene for an inquisitive 11-year-old just a month earlier! *A. W. Martin*

Right:

Over & Wharton, 2 August 1965

A Stanier Class 5, on the thrice-weekly trip from Warrington, shunts the yard. On the extreme right is the engine shed, partially destroyed by fire in 1942, and in the distance the wooden goods shed and the station buildings. On the right, beyond the railway, is the site of Liverpool salt works, demolished in the 1930s. Note the delivery lorry in the yard. The freight service ceased in June 1968, and drastic changes were about to affect the yard with the buildings and sidings removed to create space for a large stockpile of rock salt from 1966. *P. E. Baughan*

Below:

Over & Wharton, 16 June 1947

Coal tank No 6906 takes water, having worked in from Warrington, while motor tank No 6637, sub-shedded from Warrington, resides in the shed, which closed on 27 August 1947. After the 1942 fire, the building was further shortened to the rear office only. The 18-lever LNWR signalbox, then the domain of signalmen Joe Cross and Tom Sanbach, closed when 'one engine in steam' working was introduced in November 1952. The gated siding beyond led originally to Liverpool Works, closed in 1930, but was still used for coal traffic to Birkenhead Works and to reach the SU engine shed from which SU locomotives ventured onto BR tracks until c1955. *W. A. Camwell*

Above:
Over & Wharton, 16 June 1947
The last day of passenger services sees 0-6-2 tank No 6906 again, about to leave with the last train to Warrington – the one train of the day not worked by the Wharton-based motor set. Services had previously been suspended as a wartime economy between January 1917 and July 1920. After the war, competition from the vehicles of the North Western Road Car Company was severe, and there was little future for the six or so unevenly timed and inconvenient services on the branch. *W. A. Camwell*

Below:
Over & Wharton, c1920
Wharton-based LNWR 2-4-2 tank No 1458 and a single coach form one of the very infrequent departures from the station to Acton Bridge, Warrington or another South Lancashire destination, probably shortly after the wartime suspension of services from 1917 to 1920. *Lens of Sutton, T. Booth collection*

Above:
Weaver Valley, Winsford, *c*1930
This view, about half a mile north of Winsford town bridge, shows clearly the impact of the salt industry on the landscape. The river is in the centre, with the CLC branch and Over Works in the foreground. Opposite, on the east bank, is Lycett's Railway and River Works, with the 1870 line from Kays Crossing coming in across Wharton Common, top right. The earlier Lycett's connection, direct to the main line at Winsford goods yard, disappears along the edge of the tributary valley, also top right. The wagons, top left, are in sidings for Stubbs Little Meadow Works (supposedly closed in 1913, but showing some signs of activity) and the National Works. Extreme top left is Deakin's Bostock Works and the SU wagon works. Salt chutes for boat loading line the valley sides, derelict areas mark the sites of closed works, and a large brine cistern can be seen, top left. Note also how deeply the landscape is cut by tributary streams. Today both sides of the river have been landscaped and few features of this scene now remain. *Cheshire County Library*

Right:
Winsford Junction, 21 February 1967
Back at the main-line junction, the local track gang are busy as Class 5 No 44727 pulls out of the up loop in a scene once so familiar. The 'Black Fives' and their merchandise freights ran in almost constant procession in steam days, rattling along at all times of the day and night. The up loop from Verdin Sidings was abolished in 1972. *A. Wilkinson*

Left:
Winsford Junction, 10 April 1965
Class 8F No 48411 bustles past with the 05.15 Carlisle–Bushbury express freight, a return working for a Shrewsbury engine. The layout is not that different from Edwardian times except that on the left, between the crossover and Smokehall bridge in the background, there were once sidings for the SU wagon works and four salt works, Bostock, Moulton Hall, Bush's and Meadow. A down freight disappears in the distance. *A. Wilkinson*

Below:
Smokehall, 18 February 1967
North of Winsford Junction, '8F' No 48054 heads a Bamfurlong-Milford Haven up tanks, as 'Britannia' No 70016 *Ariel* blasts away from a permanent way slowing with 3L14, the 1.16pm Crewe–Carlisle parcels. The down goods siding has just been lifted and it is a far cry from the days when the area to the right was lined with salt works and Salt Union industrial locomotives bustled alongside the main line. *A. Wilkinson*

Right:
Verdin Sidings signalbox, bottom centre, and Newbridge salt works, in an LMS plan of *c*1930.

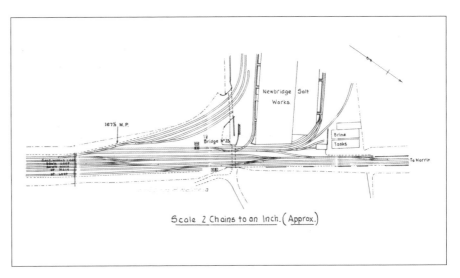

Below:
Verdin Sidings, 18 February 1967
BR Class 9F 2-10-0 No 92223, with 4L41, the 11.25 Oxley Sidings to Carlisle fitted freight, passes the 36-lever box that by this time only controlled the entry and exit to up and down loops. From 1867 there were extensive sidings on the right for Verdin's Newbridge Works. This closed in 1956, with the sidings partially used by Aerastone Ltd until about 1962. The box opened in 1898 with the new goods loops to Winsford Junction, and was abolished with the up loop on 28 August 1972. The original Verdin Sidings box was further north on the up side, close to overbridge No 27. *A. Wilkinson*

Right:
Verdin Sidings, May 1967
Winsford Verdin Grammar School's Transport Society takes an extended lunch to see the preserved 'A4' No 4498 *Sir Nigel Gresley* with the 1.16pm Carlisle parcels, *en route* to Glasgow to work a railtour to Aberdeen. With the track fettled up for high speed, the 'A4', recently overhauled at Crewe, was able to eclipse the best average 'Duchess' performance in the area. A spectacular collision here in July 1899 saw a down goods headed by coal engine No 940 over-run the loop, colliding with a down express goods hauled by 2-4-0 No 901. A Liverpool–Abergavenny excursion, with 'DX' 0-6-0 No 1243, ran into the wreckage, fortunately without fatalities. *A. Wilkinson*

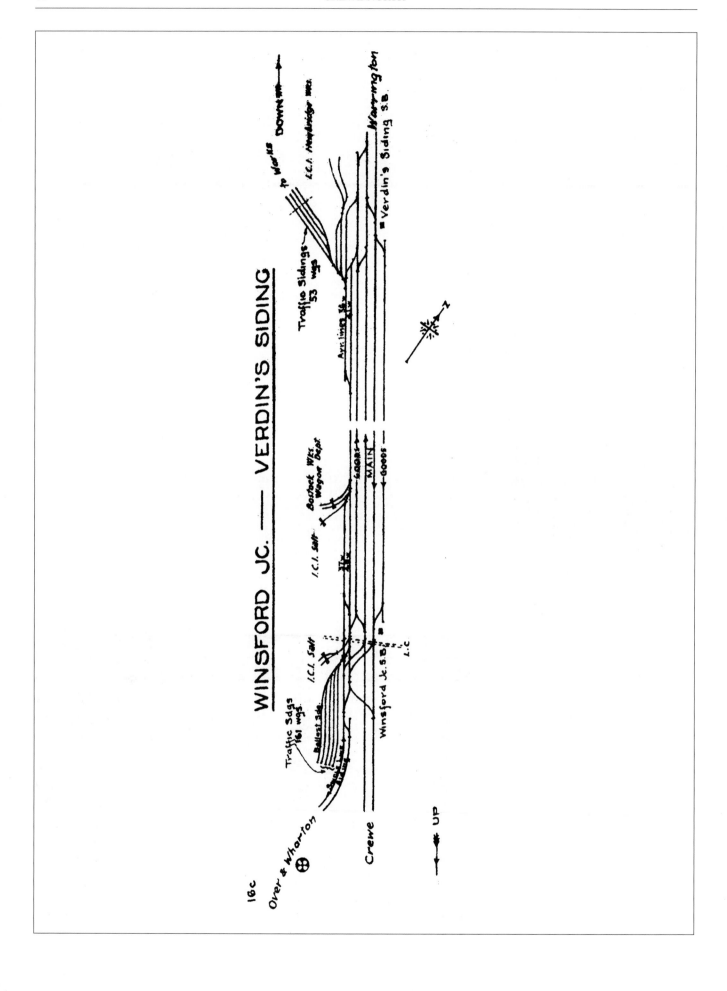

Left:
The 1948 track layout between Crewe and Weaver Junction, with an enlargement of Winsford Junction–Verdin Sidings. *Aston Collection, Kidderminster Railway Museum*

Right:
Newbridge salt works, 19 June 1934
Falcon 0-4-0ST *Winsford* of 1889 – a type popular with Verdins at their various salt works – shunted at Newbridge and other North Works until 1935, when she moved to the SU's Port Clarence Works. She is seen here probably on the Newbridge layout at Verdin Sidings, with the land to the rear dropping away sharply to the Weaver. SU industrials were allowed to use the down goods siding, and parts of the Wharton branch and Brine branch, to access the various east bank works. There were few such movements after 1950, and the Running Agreement lapsed in 1956. *J. F. Ward collection*

Left:
Verdin Sidings, *c*1947
This Salt Union gable-roofed 8-ton salt van is typical of the many that were once a familiar sight at Winsford in their red livery. The gable roof was employed to lessen the likelihood of water seepage, and such vehicles carried high-quality fine-grain salt in cartons or in uncovered 'block' format. Falks Works was on the west bank of the Weaver, served by the CLC branch, but under the SU. Products from this works for certain destinations were most probably taken across the river and loaded at Newbridge Works, as the wagon is clearly labelled 'return empty to Winsford LMS' and for repair purposes.
ICI Chemicals & Polymers Ltd

Right:
Salt Union wagon works, *c*1923
The works was located just north of Winsford Junction on the down side and is believed to have closed about 1945. Typical 10-ton wooden wagons for common salt are being repaired. The grease-lubricated axleboxes, neatly piled-up wagon springs and the immaculate condition of the workshop should be noted. *Cheshire County Museum*

9. HARTFORD AND ACTON BRIDGE

Above:

Vale Royal Viaduct, *c*1930

The River Weaver is quite deeply incised into the Cheshire Plain and its meanderings saw two impressive viaducts built by the GJR. Vale Royal, the smaller of the two, is being crossed by a Midland Compound on a down express. The five 63-foot spans, some 60 feet high, cost £40,000 and occupied 700 men for two years, with Cheshire sandstone supplied via the River Weaver. *T. Booth collection*

Below:

Hartford, *c*1910

An LNWR Class B four-cylinder 0-8-0 Compound approaches with an up freight. Being close to Northwich, and with a road connection to Tarporley, the GJR buildings were large and more ornate than at Winsford. Extensive timber buildings have been added, and the constricted site, in a long, deep cutting, involved an elaborate footbridge and walkways. Later a common booking office at road level served both platforms. The milk churns and pigeon baskets point to once important, but now long-vanished, traffic. *T. Booth collection*

Above:
Hartford, June 1957
Class 8F No 48291 trundles a down through freight past the station. The constricted site meant that goods facilities comprised only the cramped wooden goods shed and loading dock on the up side, and a horse landing behind the signalbox (which was of Saxby & Farmer design dating from 1876, when the main line was first block signalled, and was the last survivor in the area). Coal yard facilities existed at the privately owned Douglas Siding, just north of the station on the down side. The station closed to goods traffic on 17 August 1959. *H. B. Priestley*

Right:
Hartford, c1890
A Webb 'Experiment' class 2-2-2-0 compound heads an up express through the station. Note the absence of the footbridge and booking office at road level, installed after 1895. Sixty miles per hour was uncommonly good going for these sluggardly machines, which may explain why the early camera has coped exceptionally well with the speed of the train. *C. M. & J. M. Bentley collection*

Left:
Hartford, 31 July 1953
Here is a fine study of the last unrebuilt 'Royal Scot', No 46137 *The Prince of Wales's Volunteers (South Lancashire)*, as she comes through with the 10.10am Edinburgh–Birmingham. The bridge carrying the CLC Northwich–Chester line is just visible in the distance. *T. Lewis, R. W. Hinton collection*

Right:
The distinctive footbridge at Hartford, in a drawing dated February 1895.

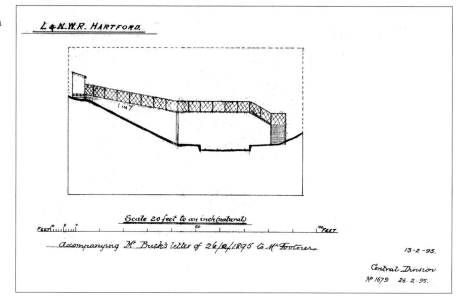

Left:
Hartford, 27 June 1953
A period scene indeed: Class 5 No 45308 approaches with what is probably the 1.30pm Barrow–Crewe, while the driver of 'Royal Scot' No 46135 *The East Lancashire Regiment* looks back for the 'right away' with the 1.35pm Euston–Blackpool Saturday service. No problems, apparently, with short platforms in those days! However, the station platforms were substantially lengthened in 1960 to accommodate full-length expresses, although today two-car Class 158s are the usual fare! *P. Astley, T. Booth collection*

Right:
Douglas Siding, Hartford, *c*1934
All is immaculate – locomotive, train, permanent way, embankments – as the pioneer Stanier Pacific No 6200 *The Princess Royal* passes Douglas Siding with the down 'Royal Scot'. The engine is almost brand new, fitted with its original straight-sided tender (and was featured on page 29 at Winsford, at the end of its career). The train is close to the point of the collision of 6 October 1944 when No 6230 *Duchess of Buccleuch* with the 9.25pm Euston–Glasgow ran through signals and into the preceding freight, fortunately without serious consequences. *L. Hobday, C. M. & J. M. Bentley collection*

Left:
Douglas Siding, Hartford, 4 August 1957
Twenty-three years later the 'Royal Scot' is equipped with BR Mark 1 standard stock in maroon livery and is in the charge of ex-Southern Railway diesels Nos 10201 and 10202, although still some four years away from regular haulage by EE Type 4s. Douglas Siding, which can be glimpsed to the right of the train, was originally an R. Evans & Co coal yard, and passed to Mr Douglas in 1890. Fletcher, Burrows & Co owned the yard in 1925, and it was leased to Lancashire United Coals, then the NCB, before closure in 1959. *A. W. Martin*

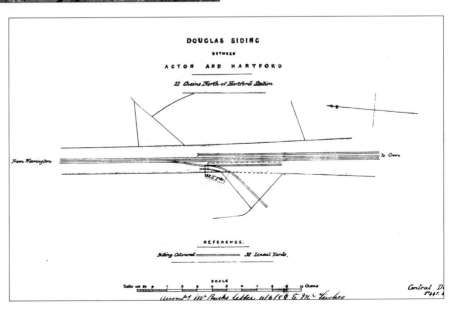

Right:
Douglas Siding: a plan dated June 1889

Above:
Douglas Siding, Hartford, 14 July 1945
Webb 2-4-2 motor-fitted tank No 6603 approaches the CLC overbridge with the late-afternoon train from Over & Wharton to Acton Bridge, where passengers had to wait almost an hour for forward services to Liverpool or Warrington. This sparse and inconvenient service had rather less than two years to live. *N. Fields*

Below:
Hodge Lane, Hartford, *c*1935
Ex-LNWR 'Claughton' 4-6-0 No 5907 *Sir Frederick Harrison* and a 'Prince of Wales' 4-6-0, double-heading a southbound express, are about to pass under the CLC Northwich–Chester line – a favourite location for enthusiasts for many years. The farm accommodation bridge in the background, close to the junction with the spur from the CLC, was demolished in 1948. *A. Wilkinson collection*

Above:
Hodge Lane, Hartford, *c*1930
A relatively unusual pairing of two ex-LNWR 0-8-0s heads a substantial unfitted up Class F express freight towards the CLC overbridge. There was then a fine array of tall LNWR signals here, which lasted until the junction was remodelled when Gorstage Yard opened in 1953.
L. Hobday, C. M. & J. M. Bentley collection

Right:
Hodge Lane, Hartford, *c*1948
The LNWR 'Claughtons' represented the end of a great and sometimes controversial line of express locomotives produced by the company. Capable of outstanding performance in skilled hands, their mechanical weaknesses saw them decimated in the 1930s with the arrival of Stanier's exceptionally reliable machines. All had gone by 1941, except No 6004 (one of the rebuilds with a larger boiler), which miraculously managed to survive, still in maroon livery, until withdrawn in 1949. The engine spent its latter years at Edge Hill, and was a frequent visitor to Cheshire, mostly on freight work. Here she heads an up express freight about to pass under the CLC route at Hartford. LNWR enthusiasts have a genuine grievance that neither a 'George V', a 'Prince of Wales' or a 'Claughton' managed to survive into preservation at this time. *J. C. Lewis*

Left:
Hodge Lane, Hartford, *c*1951
The Crewe–Liverpool locals and West of England expresses between Liverpool and Shrewsbury were often used to 'run in' ex-works locomotives. Bristol Barrow Road's 'Jubilee' No 45570 *New Zealand* passes the distinctively tall Down Outer Home signal of Hartford Junction (LNWR) with a local for Liverpool. The LNWR spur to Hartford Junction (CLC) opened in March 1870, and descends through the bridge on the left.
N. R. Knight

Below:
Hodge Lane, Hartford, 14 June 1954
This fine study shows rebuilt 'Patriot' No 45525 *Colwyn Bay* coming under the bridges carrying Hodge Lane and the CLC Chester line at the approach to Hartford Junction (LNWR) with the heavily loaded down 'Manxman'. This was a summer-only train run in connection with the Isle of Man steamers from Liverpool, and the name was carried by the 10.30am from Euston and the 2.10pm return from Lime Street. *T. Lewis, R. W. Hinton collection*

Right:

Hartford spur, 30 June 1964

Shortly before the end of steam on these workings, Northwich '8F' No 48693 brings a set of Tunstead–Wallerscote limestone hoppers down the spur towards Gorstage sidings for the Wallerscote Light Railway to ICI's Wallerscote works. The CLC Chester line is in the background. Passenger services over the spur ceased in June 1941, and it was 'put out of use' from August 1994 pending re-wiring at Hartford Junction (LNWR) box (now abolished). It re-opened in September 1997, controlled from Winsford Junction and with up access only from the slow line from Acton Bridge. The down loop from Hartford to Acton Bridge is currently disused, but is to be re-activated. *B. W. L. Brooksbank, Initial Photographics*

Left:

Hartford Junction (LNWR), c1955

The box opened in 1927 when the line to Acton Bridge was quadrupled, being built by the LMS to the late LNWR pattern. In need of re-wiring, it closed on 20 August 1994 and never re-opened, its functions being eventually transferred to Winsford Junction in 1997. Relief Signalman Harold Hodgkinson is on duty. Note the signalman's bicycle; this was an essential piece of equipment, especially for relief men who travelled considerable distances, up to 10-15 miles, by this means, even in the late 1960s. *A. Wilkinson collection*

Right:

Hartford Junction, March 1948

The LNWR junction signals frame Stephenson valve gear Class 5 No 44767, then almost brand new, heading an up Class F express freight. The 'Black Fives' were the masters of such work, then the very lifeblood of the railway. No 44767 spent some years on the Central Division, but was at Carlisle Kingmoor in 1967, provoking a poignant memory of her superb staccato pounding through Minshull Vernon with the 2.20pm Class 5 Carlisle to Crewe in that summer. Much of this traffic now moves by road or in container trains, but happily No 44767 is still with us on the North Yorkshire Moors Railway. *L&GRP*

Above:

Gorstage Yard, 15 April 1960

With Hartford Junction's signals in the background, 'Duchess' Pacific No 46238 *City of Carlisle* sprints past Gorstage Yard with a Good Friday Euston–Glasgow relief. The line was quadrupled to Acton Bridge in June 1927 when the new signalbox in the right distance replaced the original box on the up side. Hartford Junction box, the down loop and connections to Gorstage Yard were abolished from September 1997. *M. Mensing*

Below:

Gorstage Yard, 15 April 1960

The English Electric Type 4 2,000hp diesels arrived in 1959, and within two years had replaced steam on most of the principal workings. The 'Whistlers' were not then at all popular, but were in fact amongst the best of the 1955 Modernisation Plan diesels. Although rather underpowered, they did sterling work, earning fulsome praise from operators and enthusiasts alike by the time of their demise in 1984/5. No D228 is at the head of the 4.10pm Liverpool–Euston. *M. Mensing*

Right:
Gorstage Yard, *c*1953
ICI's post-war expansion at Northwich saw a doubling of rail traffic to 12,000 wagon-loads per month, mostly handled on the steeply graded, single-track Winnington branch. The Wallerscote Light Railway opened on 21 February 1953 to link the Winnington/ Wallerscote complex with the new Gorstage Yard alongside the main line. (There was also a series of trip workings to and from Northwich for eastbound traffic.) A 'Royal Scot' passes the newly opened sidings with a down express, while the light railway descends eastwards towards the works on the left. *ICI Chemicals & Polymers Ltd*

Above:
Gorstage Yard, 15 April 1960
ICI, an early user of diesels, had displaced its steam shunting fleet by 1958. Eight 150hp Ruston & Hornsbys replaced 12 Borrows well tanks, while five 250hp Yorkshire Engine Co machines supplanted seven eight-year-old Barclays. Heavy work was done by English Electric 400hp 0-6-0DEs of 1951, very similar to the BR 350hp design. *Davy*, a 400hp unit, brings empty limestone hoppers for Tunstead down the light railway alongside Gorstage sidings. *M. Mensing*

Right:
Wallerscote Light Railway, *c*1952
In this scene during the construction of the light railway, a Manning Wardle 0-6-0 saddle tank, minus buffers, busies itself with a tipping wagon. *J. C. Lewis*

Wallerscote Light Railway, *c*1953
From Gorstage, the light railway fell at 1 in 100 through a steep cutting to Avenue sidings (1¾ miles). Here a 400hp diesel descends towards Wallerscote works with 1,000 tons of limestone. The hoppers, built by Charles Roberts & Co of Wakefield from 1937, were vacuum-fitted, 39ft 5in over the buffers and 11 feet high, and ran on 6ft-wheelbase bogies, 26 feet apart. The tare weight was 22½ tons, 67 tons loaded. Sixteen-hopper trains with '8F' power made a stirring sight, and the load increased to 18 hoppers with Class 25 diesels. The hoppers, not superseded until the end of 1997, latterly ran in fewer, 22-vehicle trains with double-headed Class 37 diesels, which could equal the '8Fs' for vociferous volume when extended!
ICI Chemicals & Polymers Ltd

Below:
Wallerscote and Winnington Works, August 1965
Avenue sidings are in the right foreground, leading to Wallerscote Works, with Winnington Works in the middle distance. The Weaver Navigation is on the left, and the conveyor (top right) marks the beginning of the Winnington branch to Oakleigh sidings and the Hartford Triangle. The Anderton Boat Lift, now once again operational, is the dark mass to the left of the chimneys of Winnington Works. Wallerscote Works closed in 1983 and the light railway was lifted in 1991. Just the merest fraction of the rail traffic of the 1950s is generated by Winnington, a stark illustration of decline in rail freight traffic over the last 30 years, and also of the fortunes of that once unassailable industrial giant ICI, later Brunner, Mond Ltd, and acquired in 2007 by the Dutch firm Akzo Nobel. *ICI Chemicals & Polymers Ltd*

Right:

Acton Bridge, *c*1939
The 6½-hour prestige 'Coronation Scot' streamliner service between London and Glasgow was introduced in 1937. Here the setting sun highlights the thrilling prospect of the up train, London-bound behind No 6224 *Princess Alexandra*. Acton Bridge station's Home and Starting signals are visible in the background, while an LNWR 2-4-2 tank and motor set wait for a gap in the traffic to return with one of the infrequent local services to Warrington. *F. A. Lewis collection*

Below:

Acton Bridge signalbox, *c*1956
Signalman George Griffiths, box lad Sid Bailey and lineman Len Gleave are in attendance. The LNWR block instruments have about another four years to go before being replaced by train describers in preparation for the Liverpool electrification. This 1893 box was abolished on 25 June 1972. *T. Booth collection*

Below right:

Acton Bridge signalbox, *c*1962
District Relief Signalman Harold Hodgkinson is at work in the box after the installation of train describers in 1961. Relief men were expected to abide by the traditions of the regular men, so Harold has his slippers on! The later Inspector Hodgkinson began his career at Weaver Junction in 1938, went abroad to Germany with the Royal Engineers helping to restore order to the shattered system in the Cologne area at the end of the war, then returned to many years of signalling between Hartford and Weaver Junction, before becoming one of those essential operating supervisors 'in trilby hat and black mackintosh' who kept the railway going 24 hours per day. Railways were his life and it was a pleasure to have known him and his good wife, Alice. *A. Wilkinson collection*

Left:

Acton Bridge, *c*1914
When railways were supreme and the LNWR was the 'Premier Line', 'Claughton' No 1319 *Sir Frederick Harrison* brings the long-standing 8.30am Carlisle–Euston train into a scene full of reminders of a bygone age. Parcels, luggage in advance, pigeon baskets, milk churns and private-owner coal wagons have long disappeared, although the Railway Hotel and the typical row of LNWR railwaymen's cottages on the right still survive. *A. G. Ellis, courtesy of G. B. Ellis*

Middle left:

Acton Bridge, May 1955
Rebuilt 'Royal Scot' No 46110 *Grenadier Guardsman* muscles into the rise from Weaver Junction to Crewe with a Liverpool–Euston express. The station was rebuilt in 1925 to accommodate a longer up loop, involving new buildings on the bridge and a new up platform waiting area. In its heyday the station boasted locals to Crewe, Crewe via Northwich, Liverpool and Warrington, and motor trains to Over & Wharton, Ditton Junction and Earlestown. On the right the thrice weekly trip from Warrington appears to be calling, while the local coal merchant loads his lorry from one of the wagons in the sidings. *T. Lewis, R. W. Hinton collection*

Below:

Acton Bridge, 27 April 1951
Webb 2-4-2 tank No 46701 stands in the yard with a motor train from Warrington. Although Preston Brook and Moore closed after the war, a skeleton service to St Helens and Earlestown still connected spasmodically with Liverpool–Crewe locals. Theoretically dieselised from January 1961, the service was often a Warrington or St Helens Ivatt Class 2 tank and motor set until final withdrawal in June 1965. *H. C. Casserley*

Above:

Acton Bridge, 27 March 1957

The spring sunlight catches Edge Hill's 'Jubilee' No 45681 *Aboukir* as she bursts under the station bridge with a down 'Empress Voyager' ocean liner special from Euston to Liverpool Riverside. Such trains ran to regular provisional paths in the timetable and continued until air competition finally banished the wonderful transatlantic liners from the Mersey in the early 1970s. Note the oil lamp under the bridge – an entirely usual form of illumination at many stations until well into the 1970s! *T. Lewis*

Right:

Acton Bridge, 1938

An up through freight approaches, headed by rebuilt 'Claughton' No 5946 *Duke of Connaught*. On the right is Moulton's Siding, another R. Evans & Co coal yard, which closed in the late 1950s. The station goods yard closed on 4 January 1965, all connections being removed on 6 March 1966.

J. G. Muir, courtesy of The Railway Magazine

10. WEAVER JUNCTION

Left:
Cliff Lane underbridge, *c*1956
Edge Hill's 'Jubilee' No 45647 *Sturdee* forges away from Dutton Viaduct with an up afternoon express. From the 'scratch' look of the coaches, it is possibly an up ocean liner special from Liverpool Riverside to Euston. Note the fine LNWR Weaver Junction Down Distant signals on the left. *BR, T. Booth collection*

Below:
Cliff Lane underbridge, 2 April 1968
After the closure of Crewe South and Warrington depots in the autumn of 1967, and that at Northwich in March 1968, the last regular steam workings were those of Speke Junction and Heaton Mersey engines between Weaver Junction and Hartford Junction on freight traffic for ICI's plants at Runcorn, which ceased with the closure of those two depots in May 1968. On a fine spring afternoon, '8F' No 48684 makes valedictory progress southwards with Runcorn–Worksop empties. *A. Wilkinson*

Above:

Dutton Viaduct, *c*1907
The broad Weaver valley must have presented a formidable obstacle to the
pioneer railway builders of the mid-1830s. Their response was
impressive: a sandstone viaduct of 20 arches of 63-foot span taking the
railway boldly across the valley at a height of 65 feet. The design was
George Stephenson's, with final construction by Joseph Locke; the
contractor was David McIntosh of London, and it took two years to build
at a cost of £54,000. Today, 170-plus years later, it is carrying far heavier
and faster trains than its builders could ever have envisaged. An LNWR
2-4-0 heads an up stopping train across the impressive and finely detailed
structure. The sandstone came from a quarry in the nearby Cheshire
Ridge, brought in via the River Weaver. *T. Booth collection*

Right:

Dutton Viaduct, July 1960
Photographed from Weaver Junction box, 'Jubilee' No 45721
Impregnable comes off the viaduct with down special W691. The box was
remote and access was difficult – reached through two farmyards from an
obscure stretch of road – and some signalmen preferred to wait for a gap
in the traffic and walk across the viaduct to get into work. Note the superb
LNWR Down Home signals. *N. Jones*

Right:

Dutton Viaduct, July 1960
Horwich 'Crab' '5MT' 2-6-0 No 42881 brings
down excursion W621 across the viaduct.
Ruggedly strong and reliable, the 'Crabs' could
stand in for a 'Black Five' on fitted freight and
passenger work without the slightest qualm and
were very much part of the West Coast scene
from their introduction in 1926 to the mid-
1960s. Note the length of the viaduct and the
apparent lack of safety recesses, which made it
a dangerous place for track-workers. *N. Jones*

Above:
Weaver Junction, 1954
The tall LNWR signalbox, standing guard at the north end of Dutton Viaduct, is being passed by Carnforth's 'Super D' 0-8-0 No 49282, fresh from overhaul, on an up through freight. *T. Lewis, N. E. Preedy collection*

Left:
Weaver Junction, 1938
A streamlined 'Duchess' heads south with the up 'Coronation Scot'. The photographer was Harold Hodgkinson, who as box lad was just beginning a long and fruitful railway career. The high-speed turnouts between the Liverpool and Warrington lines were the scene of the derailment of the leading coupled wheels of 'Royal Scot' No 6131 *Planet* on the down 'Midday Scot' on 7 July 1930. A new signal box opened in 1962 on the up side, just north of the bridge in the background, but in September 1997 its functions were taken over by the 1898 LNWR box at Winsford Junction.
H. Hodgkinson

Right:

Weaver Junction, 1938
'Royal Scot' No 6142 *The York & Lancaster Regiment*, at the head of a fine set of the latest LMS coaches, sweeps down from the Birdswood flyover on the up Liverpool line to join the West Coast route with a Liverpool–Euston express. *SLS No 18511, F. A. Lewis collection*

Middle right:

Weaver Junction, c1958
In their latter years the '5XP' 'Patriot' 4-6-0s spent much of their time on fitted freight work. No 45544 lays a smokescreen across the surroundings as she brings a heavy Class E express freight southwards on the up Warrington line, with the up Liverpool on the embankment to the right. The 'Patriots' continued affectionately wuffling away on such work until the last survivors were withdrawn from Carnforth in the late summer of 1962. *A. C. Gilbert, T. Booth collection*

Below:

Birdswood flyover, 28 June 1957
'Duchess' No 46253 *City of St Albans* sweeps across the up Liverpool flyover with the 16-coach 'Red Rose', the 5.25pm Liverpool–Euston 'flyer'. On the left, the down Liverpool line climbs towards Sutton Weaver, while the signals belong to Birdswood box, behind the train, which controlled traffic on both lines and a refuge siding on the up Warrington, just beyond the flyover. The box was abolished with the opening of the new Weaver Junction box in 1962. *R. J. Blenkinsop*

11. NORTH TOWARDS WARRINGTON

Above:

Preston Brook, 25 July 1959
The pioneer 'Royal Scot', No 46100, heads the up 'Lakes Express' from Workington, Keswick and Windermere to Euston. The appearance of this heavy seasonal service always marked the beginning of the Summer Timetable, and until 1963 it was invariably a job for a 'Converted Scot' or 'Patriot'. Preston Brook signalbox, closed on 13 March 1961, is in the distance, with the goods yard hidden by the rear of the train and the station just round the corner in the far distance. *J. A. Peden, T. Booth collection*

Left:

Preston Brook, 1 March 1911
The GJR stations here and at Moore were even more basic than at Winsford or Minshull Vernon. This small station provided the original access to Runcorn, and a road connection ran from the impressive, adjacent Red Lion hotel until the direct Liverpool line opened in 1869. There was also an important interchange with the nearby Trent & Mersey and Bridgewater canals. From 1852 to 1863 a connection ran from the nearby Birkenhead Joint line at Norton to a warehouse on the canal to avoid the LNWR's blocking of goods traffic for Manchester at Warrington. The station closed to passengers on 1 March 1948 and to goods on 1 September 1958. *Lens of Sutton*

Right:
Preston Brook, 4 August 1947
Here is a fine study of one of the many GJR overbridges constructed from local sandstone from the Cheshire Ridge, which have now all fallen foul of electrification clearances. Showing all the signs of post-war 'maintenance', No 6211 *Queen Maud* bursts through the arch with an up express. In the background is the fine double-arched aqueduct carrying the Bridgewater Canal's Runcorn branch, which was replaced in 1972 for the 1974 electrification. *W. D. Cooper*

Left:
Preston Brook, 1 April 1967
Class 5 No 45259 is about to pass under the Bridgewater Canal with a very substantial up express freight, probably 4H22, the 05.00 Carlisle–Banbury. Norton Crossing is in the distance, with a '9F' 2-10-0 heading a westbound freight on the Birkenhead Joint line on the horizon. It is amazing how much of this traffic (which admittedly needed a revolution in handling methods) has now disappeared from the railways as apparently uneconomic, provoking little sympathy for cries of congestion on the roads or for successive transport policies. *A. Wilkinson*

Right:
Norton Crossing, 14 September 1954
The box lay in open country where Red Brow Road crossed the line, and also had a clear view of trains on the Birkenhead Joint line embankment in the background, which is about to cross the main line before rejoining it at Acton Grange Junction. The small LNWR cabin became a barrier box with colour lights in 1962, and a gate box only when Warrington power box opened ten years later. The crossing closed on 10 February 1982, and the box finally closed on 13 November 1983 when public demand saw a bridleway crossing re-instated and protected by miniature lights for pedestrian traffic. Polmadie 'Royal Scot' No 46104 *Scottish Borderer* comes south on the lodging turn to Crewe, the 10.05am Glasgow–Birmingham. *T. Lewis, N. E. Preedy collection*

Left:
Moore, 15 May 1948
'Royal Scot' No 6110 *Grenadier Guardsman* comes south with W356, the 8.35am Carlisle–Crewe parcels (the 'Horse and Cart'). Almost always a heavy train, this cleared all outstanding van traffic for Crewe and points south, an institution from LNWR days until well into the 1970s; its name originated from the horses and carts that met the train in Victorian times. Moore station is in the background, with the water softening plant on the skyline. *J. D. Darby*

Right:
Moore, *c*1947
The original GJR buildings are evident on the down side as Class 5 No 4862 hurries by with a down through freight. Standard Crewe prefabricated wooden buildings do duty on the up side, which is dominated by the tower of the water softening plant. The station closed with the Wharton branch in January 1917, re-opening in February 1919 and closing temporarily in January 1943 before final closure in April 1949, hence the rather dilapidated aspect. There was no goods yard, but an up siding was provided for sludge tenders from the softening plant, which the Wharton pick-up conveyed to Warrington for Ince Moss Tip. *Stations UK*

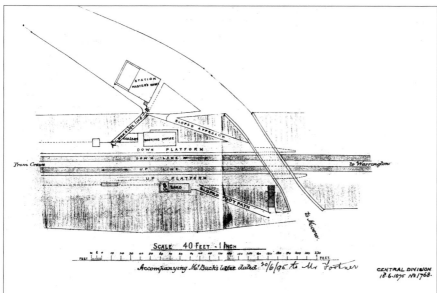

Left:
A plan of Moore station dated June 1895.

Above:

Moore, 29 March 1959

Scudding shadows chase No 46201 *Princess Elizabeth* as she hurries down the 1 in 135 from the Manchester Ship Canal bridge at Acton Grange Junction with the 10.05am Glasgow–Birmingham and Plymouth. Below on the right is the original pre-1893 alignment before the line was raised to clear the canal. The junction with the Chester line, on the right, was moved south of the bridge in 1940, hence the ARP-style signalbox on the skyline. The down line saw an unfortunate accident in July 1966 when the rear portion of a Northwich–Ravenhead freight broke away and collided with the ill-fated EE Type 4 No D322 heading the down 'Ulster Express' for Heysham. Happily, No 6201, devotedly cared for by the Locomotive 6201 Princess Elizabeth Society, is still with us, recently keeping the spirit of steam very much alive throughout the West Coast route and beyond. *T. Lewis, R. W. Hinton collection*

Right:

Acton Grange Junction, summer 1954

One of the delights of summer Saturdays in the 1950s was the appearance of Birmingham Monument Lane Compounds on extras to North Wales and the Fylde Coast. This is believed to be No 41090 regaining the main line having probably been diverted onto the Chester lines from Walton New Junction with the 11-coach 3.40pm Blackpool–Birmingham Saturday service. The fireman is clearly making preparations for an energetic run to Crewe! *F. Wemyss-Smith, M. S. Welch collection*

Left:
Acton Grange Junction, summer 1954
For many years Stoke depot boasted an extensive allocation of '4F' 0-6-0s (the 'Stoke Scots'), but usually turned out a 'Black Five' or 'Crab' 2-6-0 for long-distance excursions. On this occasion motive power must be tight and sympathies lie with the crew as they coax No 44385 along the main line with a return excursion from Blackpool to the Potteries. She is still 'just feathering' at the safety valves, and they are no doubt having a lively and dusty ride – a contrast to smart Class 5 No 45350, first choice for these workings in their last summer of steam, 1967. *F. Wemyss-Smith, M. S. Welch collection*

Below:
Acton Grange Junction, 27 July 1963
The converted '7P' 4-6-0s formed the absolute backbone of West Coast passenger power in the 1950s, performing wonders with heavy, 15-coach trains that should really have been powered by Pacifics. By the mid-1960s they were largely confined to relief work, except for the up and down 'Lakes Express', and all were withdrawn by the end of 1965. Here No 45523 *Bangor* heads 1A32, a relief to the 8.40am from Carlisle to Euston. *G. Kaye*

Right:
Acton Grange, 5 June 1954
Tredegar's 'Super D' No 49133, running in after overhaul at Crewe, comes up the 1 in 69 gradient from Walton Old Junction towards the Ship Canal bridge with an up through freight from Extension Sidings to Basford Hall.
T. Lewis, R. W. Hinton collection

Left:
Walton Sidings, Warrington, 11 March 1967
Winsford Verdin Grammar School's Transport Society is enjoying a brake-van trip from Northwich behind Class '8F' No 48151, which is tackling the gradient between Walton Old and Acton Grange junctions with the moderately loaded 8F19, the 5.48pm Extension Sidings–Northwich transfers. The Ship Canal bridge is on the horizon, with the Acton Grange Home signal beyond; the main line is on the right, with Walton Old Sidings below. No 48151 was one of the best '8Fs' at Northwich, and as a preserved locomotive has had many opportunities to demonstrate just what a versatile mixed-traffic as well as a freight locomotive the Stanier '8F' was. *A. Wilkinson*

Right:
Walton New Junction, 17 September 1966
Signalled for the up main line, Stanier '8F' No 48114 crosses the Mersey Viaduct and forges past the junction with an up banana special, probably from Preston Docks. *W. A. Brown*

12. WARRINGTON BANK QUAY

A brief history

The Warrington & Newton Railway was authorised on 14 May 1829 to link the Liverpool & Manchester Railway (then under construction) at Newton with the town of Warrington, some 5 miles to the south. The line opened on 25 July 1831 and consisted of two branches at its southern end. The branch to Dallam Lane had become a coal yard by 1850 and remained so until its closure in the early 1960s. The other branch terminated on the north side of the turnpike road at Bank Quay, where it was well placed to form the basis of future railway communication to the south.

The Grand Junction Railway was authorised on 3 May 1833 to link the W&N at Bank Quay with Birmingham. It absorbed the W&N in June 1835 and made an end-on junction with it at Bank Quay. It then absorbed several strategically placed railways in South Lancashire before becoming a major constituent of the LNWR when that company was formed on 16 July 1846. The main line to the north was extended to Wigan in 1832, Preston in 1838 and Lancaster by 1840. Through coaches began to run from Liverpool to London via Warrington in 1838, the line to Carlisle opened on 17 December 1846, and a London–Glasgow service began two years later. Apart from the obvious benefit of trunk hauls to distant markets, the coming of the railway provided a significant boost to the local economy, linking the chemical industries of mid-Cheshire and South Lancashire with the South Lancashire coalfield. Crosfields chemical plant at Bank Quay, the Bank Quay foundry and Bank Quay glass works all flourished at this time, while until at least the 1870s Richard Evans of Haydock Colliery worked his own trains over the GJR to serve his lineside coal depots and salt interests in Winsford.

In June 1846 the Birkenhead, Lancashire & Cheshire Junction Railway was authorised to link Hooton with Heaton Norris, with branches from Helsby to Chester, to the GJR at Warrington, and a continuation from Warrington to the Manchester South Junction & Altrincham Railway at Timperley. Twelve months later the company was absorbed by the Chester & Birkenhead Railway, which had opened in 1840. The LNWR's response was to offer to convey Cheshire Junction traffic to

Manchester, and the Timperley extension was consequently abandoned. The Cheshire Junction, which joined the LNWR at Walton Junction, immediately south of the Mersey, opened from Chester on 18 December 1850 with a service of four daily passenger trains to and from Manchester Victoria. Matters were much less amicable on the freight side, for the LNWR deliberately delayed goods for Manchester at Walton, especially if they originated on the LNWR's bitter rival, the Shrewsbury & Chester! Matters became so bad that in 1852 the S&C obtained powers for a line from Norton station to the Bridgewater Canal at Preston Brook for transhipment to Manchester, which opened in 1853. To add fuel to the fire, in 1854 the S&C was absorbed by the LNWR's arch rival, the GWR.

In 1847 the St Helens Railway was authorised to extend from Runcorn Gap to Warrington, ultimately passing under the LNWR at Bank Quay to connect with the Cheshire Junction line. It opened to a temporary station at Litton Mill on 1 February 1853, prompting a revival – the Warrington & Altrincham Railway, linking the St Helens Railway at Warrington with the MSJ&A at Timperley. The W&A opened to a joint station with the St Helens Railway at Warrington Arpley on 1 May 1854, and a connection from Arpley to Walton Junction was opened on 8 November 1855 after months of squabbling with the LNWR over signalling arrangements.

The W&A had also obtained powers for a controversial extension from Timperley to Stockport. The MSJ&A was unhappy about conveying the W&A's traffic onwards to Manchester, and the LNWR refused to allow GWR freight traffic over its lines into the city. The Warrington & Stockport and GWR were forced to build a goods shed at Broadheath, and traffic over the W&S did not begin until 1 October 1856. From February 1858 the Manchester Sheffield & Lincolnshire Railway made use of the W&S and St Helens Railway to introduce a Garston to King's Cross service via Manchester London Road, in competition with the LNWR's trains from Liverpool to Euston (timings were comparable since the LNWR's direct line through Runcorn did not open until 1869). In 1859 the W&S proposed a Chester–

Warrington Arpley service to connect with the King's Cross trains, prompting a frosty response from the LNWR, which banned the W&S from Chester General!

Eventually, in 1859, after the resignation of Captain Huish, the LNWR sought more amicable relations with its neighbours. It absorbed the W&S in 1861 and the St Helens Railway two years later, and granted the GWR running powers into Manchester Liverpool Road in November 1858. In 1859 the Cheshire Junction became the Birkenhead Railway, which in 1860 passed into the joint control of the GWR and LNWR. On 1 July 1863 the line from Helsby to Hooton was opened, significantly shortening the route to Birkenhead docks. These developments rendered the S&C's Norton branch redundant and the rails were lifted about 1880, although the S&C's canalside warehouse at Preston Brook survived until destroyed by fire in 1961. The opening of the Weaver Junction–Ditton Junction line in 1869 also ended the exchange of passengers and goods for Runcorn at Preston Brook, although the Bridgewater Canal Siding there remained in use until about 1958.

In 1868 the LNWR opened a new station at Bank Quay to the south of the original establishment and including platforms for the Low Level line. The imposing Warrington Arpley station, half a mile to the east and quite convenient for the town, was then closed on 16 November 1868, but re-opened on 2 October 1871 following a public outcry. In the meantime the route from Skelton Junction to Stockport had been opened on 1 August 1866, establishing an invaluable freight by-pass route around south Manchester that was to keep the Low Level line through Warrington busy until the 1980s.

With the Lancashire coalfield to the north, a large area of flat land bounded by the Sankey Navigation, River Mersey and Manchester Ship Canal, and well served by both the LNWR routes, encouraged much local heavy industry in the vicinity of Bank Quay and outwards towards the Ship Canal,

Right:
The 1948 track layout from Weaver Junction to Warrington and beyond, with an enlargement of the Warrington district. *Aston Collection, Kidderminster Railway Museum*

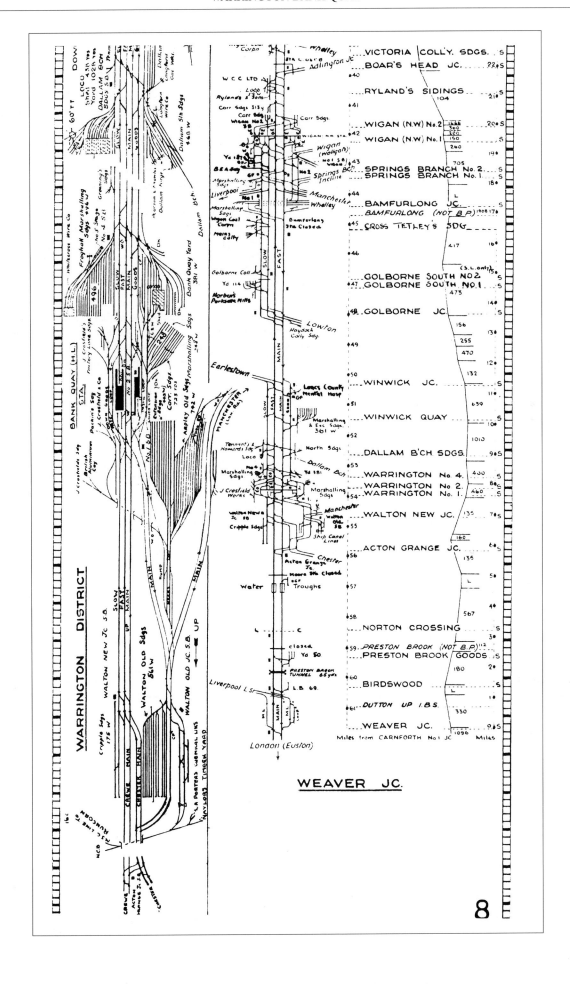

WARRINGTON DISTRICT

WEAVER JC.

which opened in 1893. The Ship Canal Company also took care to develop industry along its banks and established its own railway system, feeding into the LNWR at Walton Old Junction, being principally concerned with R. Evans & Co's pit prop and timber yard, and the Laporte Chemicals plant. Numerous other plants opened in the vicinity of the Low Level line, and with the Birkenhead Joint Line able to tap into port traffic, general goods from the south and west via Shrewsbury and Chester, and a developing petro-chemical industry in south Merseyside, Warrington was very much a developing freight traffic centre by the turn of the century.

The coming of the Manchester Ship Canal had a significant physical impact on the local railways. Both the LNWR main line and the Low Level line had to be carried across the waterway at a height of some 70 feet, involving the abandonment of the original alignments and new routeings with a standard gradient of 1 in 135 on either side of massively engineered bowstring girder bridges. On the south side, the Crewe and Chester routes were diverted from 9 July 1893 to connect just south of the new Acton Grange Viaduct. The old Crewe line alignment is still partially visible from the train today to the east of the present main line, while the old Chester alignment was for many years a 'cripple' siding from its junction with the new line at Daresbury, but is now abandoned. On the north side of the canal, a new Mersey Bridge at a much higher level than the old 'Twelve Arches' viaduct of the GJR was needed. Immediately north of this bowstring bridge, of similar size and design to Acton Grange Viaduct, was Walton New Junction, between the Crewe and Chester lines, which opened on 16 April 1894. The previous Walton Junction, between the original routes, then became Walton Old Junction. A new alignment on a 1 in 69 gradient connected Walton Old and Acton Grange Junctions to provide a route for freight traffic to and from Arpley

yards or for traffic heading eastwards via the Arpley spur. From 1900 new marshalling yards were developed at Arpley, between the Arpley spur and the line from Bank Quay to 'Twelve Arches'. The original Warrington & Stockport Railway route in the vicinity was lifted and the W&S viaduct across the Mersey just east of the 'Twelve Arches' was dismantled for wartime scrap in 1940.

Local industries continued to establish rail connections in the years leading to the Second World War. British Aluminium set up a plant close to Bank Quay station in 1903, while Crosfields chemical works expanded substantially throughout the period. Thames Board Mills set up a plant in 1937 with a large railway system, which had been abandoned by the 1980s in favour of road haulage. A similar story applied to the Laporte Chemicals establishment of 1946 served by the MSC Railway, which had itself closed by the late 1970s. Local industry also flourished alongside the Low Level line, particularly in the vicinity of Sankey Bridges, but few of these plants were still using rail by the mid-1970s. Through working of Great Western trains and locomotives to Manchester came to an end with nationalisation in 1948, after which the trains still ran, but with London Midland motive power. However, in steam days to 1968, Warrington remained a very busy freight centre with many trip freights serving local industry and making transfers between the yards at Bank Quay, Arpley, Froghall Sidings, the Dallam branch and the St Helens area, where the glass industry was firmly established – a large allocation of Midland Class 3F 0-6-0s being based at Warrington Dallam and its sub-shed at Arpley for these workings in the early 1960s.

On the passenger front, Warrington tended to be served by 'second line' main-line trains destined for Carlisle, Furness or the Fylde, but remained nevertheless a busy centre. An important secondary traffic flow was from Manchester and points east to

North Wales, with heavy excursion traffic during the summer months. Local services were once prolific to South Lancashire towns, invariably provided by a fleet of motor trains powered by Webb 5ft 6in 2-4-2 tanks, and Ivatt Class 2 2-6-2 tanks after the war. The service to Northwich was a wartime casualty, disappearing in 1941. The Bolton service survived until 1954, and services to Earlestown and St Helens, partially dieselised, for a further ten years. On the Low Level line, the imposing but neglected Arpley station was finally closed from 15 September 1958, being demolished ten years later. Passenger services between Ditton Junction and Manchester Oxford Road were withdrawn from 1 September 1962.

Freight traffic on the main line remained prolific until the early 1970s when much rationalisation followed. A subtle change in traffic patterns saw Arpley yards assume the much more important role of assembling traffic from the South and North West and redistributing it throughout the North and Scotland, largely at the expense of Crewe's Basford Hall Yard, which was much rationalised from 1972. The same year saw the opening of Warrington power signalbox and the end of semaphore signalling in the area. On the Low Level line, petro-chemical traffic to the North East had been building up steadily since the mid-1960s – the Stanlow–Leeds petrol trains, double-headed sometimes by two '9F' 2-10-0s being a particularly fond memory. By the late 1970s there was space to divert much of this traffic to other routes, while the other major flow of trans-Pennine coal traffic was much reduced, especially after the closure of the Woodhead route in 1981, while the line between Skelton Junction and Arpley was closed from 8 July 1985. However, part of the line is still open at Warrington, providing run-round facilities for the block coal trains to Fiddlers Ferry power station, which now reach Warrington from a variety of directions.

Right:

Extension Sidings, 11 March 1967
Class 8F No 48151 sets back for the 5.48pm freight to Northwich as a Class 9F 2-10-0 passes on the line from Arpley to Walton Old and Acton Grange junctions with a Leeds–Stanlow empty tanks haul. *A. Wilkinson*

Right:

Extension Sidings, 11 March 1967
Class 8F No 48151 is ready to leave with the Northwich freight, with the Arpley-Walton Old Junction line on the far right. The gentleman in the foreground is one of the yard foremen, who was retiring on that day, while the Northwich crew look on from the engine cab. *A. Wilkinson*

Left:

Warrington Arpley shed, 2 October 1960
This substantial two-road shed opened in 1854 to service engines working on the Low Level line, leased by the LNWR from 1859. Subsequently a sub-shed of Warrington Dallam, it serviced freight locomotives working into Walton yards and those on the Ditton Junction–Manchester London Road passengers, assuming major responsibility for the motor trains on this service from Sutton Oak shed in 1961/2. The very small allocation for these trains ranged from LNWR 2-4-2 and 0-6-2 tanks, the L&YR 2-4-2 version, and most modern LMS tank varieties, with Ivatt Class 2 tanks finally. There was a turntable, latterly disused, and a 'tank over' coaling stage. Stanier '8F' No 48536 and classmates, together with 'WD' 2-8-0s, rest between duties, with '3F' 0-6-0s and tanks for local trip working. The shed closed on 27 May 1963. *H. G. Ballantyne*

Left:
**Warrington Bank Quay Low Level,
1 September 1962**
Ivatt Class 2 2-6-2 tank No 41211 heads a three-coach LMS motor set forming the 4.18pm to Manchester Oxford Road on the last day of services between Ditton Junction and Manchester. Although most local services in the Warrington area were dieselised by this time, at least one LMS motor set remained active in the Warrington/St Helens area, covering for non-available multiple units, until 1966.
B. W. L. Brooksbank, Initial Photographics

Below:
Warrington south, 5 October 1962
Rebuilt 'Patriot' No 45545 *Planet* darkens the sky as she makes a vigorous start on the 1 in 135 from Bank Quay with the 4.30pm Manchester Exchange–Llandudno 'Club' train. This, together with the Southport and Blackpool 'Club' trains – prime commuter services for the business community when introduced in Edwardian times – still commanded special attention (note the smart BR standard stock), but rapidly lost their exclusiveness when DMUs took over from 1966/7. Arpley sidings are on the right, with Warrington No 1 box in the distance and a GPO set-down point for the 'West Coast Postal' on the left – another vanished feature of the current railway scene. *J. R. Carter*

Right:

Warrington Bank Quay, 1 June 1949
Included as a tribute to the years of service put in by the Webb 5ft 6in 2-4-2 tanks on motor train services in the area, which once extended to Northwich, Over & Wharton, Crewe, Earlestown, St Helens and various South Lancashire destinations, No 6628 passes No 1 box with a northbound motor. The first coach was originally an eight-compartment 3rd Corridor built in 1908-10, later converted to a 57-foot Luggage 3rd. The 57-foot Driving Trailer 3rd dates from 1913. *W. H. Whitworth, A. Wilkinson collection*

Right:

Warrington Bank Quay, 17 August 1963
'Eh by gum, we're off to t'seaside!' Class 5 No 45426 rolls into Bank Quay with just one of the plethora of extras, excursions and reliefs heading for the Fylde Coast on a typical summer Saturday – the 9.40am Stoke–Blackpool North – watched by a discreet group of locospotters. Warrington No 1 box is on the left.
B. W. L. Brooksbank, Initial Photographics

Below:

Warrington Bank Quay, 17 August 1963
In the 1960s Warrington was still a very busy freight centre, with local industry generating many trip workings and shunting duties, for which Dallam shed had a large allocation of '3F' 0-6-0s. 'Jinty' 0-6-0 tank No 47531 is on the freight underpass from Arpley Sidings to Bank Quay with a very mixed transfer freight, probably heading for Froghall Sidings. Included in the make-up is an ex-LNWR tender doing duty as a sludge-carrier, en route to Ince Moss Tip. *B. W. L. Brooksbank, Initial Photographics*

Above:
Warrington Bank Quay, 1926
Early LMS days at Warrington: 'Claughton' No 210 heads an up express while a Webb 2-4-2 tank stands alongside with a connecting local. Three years after the Grouping, the former would appear to be still in LNWR livery with the LNWR crest on the splasher – Crewe was notably reluctant to paint its passenger engines in LMS maroon (aka Midland Red!) unless absolutely compelled to do so. *C. M. & J. M. Bentley collection*

Below:
Warrington Bank Quay, 24 August 1935
A fine study at the north end of the station of rebuilt 'Claughton' No 5975 *Talisman*. Although capable performers, it had been impossible to eradicate all the mechanical problems with the engines and even the rebuilt 'Claughtons' disappeared rapidly with the arrival of the new Stanier locomotives. All the original machines had gone by the end of the year, and the rebuilds by 1941, except No 6004; saved by the war, she lasted until 1949. Crosfields chemical plant forms the background, and also an interesting array of signals. *C. M. & J. M. Bentley collection*

Right:
Warrington Bank Quay, 1939
'Patriot' No 5503 *The Leicestershire Regiment* arrives with W254, the 10.30am Workington–Euston – those preparing the engine have made certain that the signalmen know exactly which train it is! Note the typically solidly built and carefully detailed LNWR station water tank on the right. *C. M. & J. M. Bentley collection*

Below:
Warrington Bank Quay, 4 June 1957
Polmadie's No 46230 *Duchess of Buccleuch* sweeps through the station with the 10.05am Glasgow–Birmingham. The LMS Stanier Brake 3rd, with roof board reversed, appears to be strengthening the two BR standard vehicles forming the Glasgow–Plymouth through coaches at the head of the train. Note the LMS running-in board on the right and the LNWR water column and starting signals on the down platform, which disappeared when it was lengthened in the early 1960s. *R. J. Buckley, Initial Photographics*

Left:
Warrington Bank Quay, 15 April 1966
In the 1960s the station platforms were lengthened, buildings rebuilt and awnings cut back in preparation for the Glasgow electrification, which did not happen until 1974. Shrewsbury's '8F' No 48221 is returning home with the 05.15 Carlisle–Bushbury Class E.
A. Wilkinson

Left:
Warrington Bank Quay, 15 April 1966
Driver Quimey of Crewe Bungalow peers back for the 'right away' on a raw spring afternoon, in charge of ex-works 'Britannia' No 70038 *Robin Hood* with the 10.35 Euston–Carlisle. The modern BR water column, and particularly its brazier, appear incongruous against the new colour light Starting signal. *A. Wilkinson*

Right:
Warrington Bank Quay, *c*1945
The Great Western influence at Warrington dated from 1858 when the LNWR buried its differences with the Warrington & Chester Railway and granted the GWR running powers to Manchester Liverpool Road. The latter operated freight trains to Manchester, and joint passenger services with the LNWR/LMS. The use of GWR locomotives beyond Chester ceased with nationalisation in 1948, when the LMR resumed responsibility for the workings. Churchward 2-6-0 No 5369 and a brake-van, devoid of a back working, are seen returning to Chester through Warrington. Warrington No 2 signalbox is prominent in the background.
A. Wilkinson collection

Above:

Warrington Bank Quay, 10 August 1935

'Eh by gum, we're off to t'other seaside this time!' Holiday excursion, LMS-style: special W379 from Eccles to Llandudno arrives in pre-'Black Five' days behind LNWR Whale 19-inch goods 4-6-0 No 8749. Crosfield's plant provides the background, and the private-owner wagon in the siding is from the Florence Coal & Iron Company, Longton, Stoke-on-Trent. *C. M. & J. M. Bentley collection*

Below:

Warrington Bank Quay, 17 October 1953

Willesden's recently ex-works '8F' No 48665 with an up through freight is signalled along the goods lines to the east of the station. There are still some adjustments required, judging by the steam leak under the cab! The station goods yard is on the right, and is now the inevitable car park. *B. K. B. Green, Initial Photographics*

Left:
Warrington Dallam shed, *c*1910
The GJR set up an 'engine house' at Bank Quay, but not until 1888 did the parsimonious LNWR provide a standard 'northlight'-pattern shed for 40 locomotives together with a 42-foot, later 65-foot, turntable, about a mile north of the station. Mostly concerned with freight and local passengers, Dallam engines radiated on all LNWR routes from the town, and according to Ahrons contained 'many crocks', albeit clearly very clean and well maintained in this photograph! Lined up are 'Cauliflower' 0-6-0s for mixed traffic, many 'coal engines' and 'coal tanks', and a Class B 0-8-0. *B. Matthews collection*

Left:
Warrington Dallam shed, *c*1925
In this LMS scene, LNWR freight types, particularly 0-8-0s, still predominate, although interlopers such as an L&YR 0-8-0 and, more remarkably, a Caledonian 0-6-0 are to be seen, while an LNWR 4-4-0 takes centre stage. The extensive coal stockpile is a reflection of the industrial disputes in mining at that time. The skyline of factory chimneys, now long gone, was typical of contemporary industrial towns. Coded 23 under the LNWR and 8B from 1935 until closure, the shed housed 60 locomotives, reverting to 40 latterly. Two sub-sheds, at Over & Wharton and Arpley, closed in 1947 and 1963 respectively. *A. Wilkinson collection*

Below left:
Warrington Bank Quay, 26 September 1964
If any one steam locomotive class could embody the spirit of the West Coast route, for your author it would have to be Stanier's 'Duchesses'. Massively handsome, fast and powerful, and that beat – so deep and yet so sharp. Only spasmodically did operating conditions allow their real potential to be exploited – at maximum power they were too much for one fireman, so they were moderately timed and could be replaced with EE Type 4s or the cheaper-to-run 'Britannias'. Nevertheless, it was an incredible shock when all the survivors were withdrawn in September 1964, leaving only Crewe's No 46256 *Sir William A. Stanier FRS* a final day's outing with the RCTS 'Scottish Lowlander' special to Carlisle. Your 16-year-old author worked for three days in the slaughterhouse at Winsford Bacon Factory to raise the fare. It was an utterly captivating occasion – long will I remember the acoustics on Grayrigg and Shap! – but also beset with some of the usual West Coast operating delays. Here the maroon Pacific stands at Warrington, ready to challenge the Northern Fells for the last time; I hope the young locospotter on the platform appreciated the significance of the occasion! *J. R. Carter*